MW00627067

For Better or For Worse

FOR BETTER OR FOR WORSE

Author: Stephen Davey
Editor: Jarl K. Waggoner
Cover Design and Body Layout: Kristin Preston

CONTENTS

Chapter 1

SUBMITTING TO A SINNER

1 Peter 3:1a

One of the most recognizable songs on the planet is the wedding march, or "Bridal Chorus," an opera tune written in 1850 by composer Richard Wagner. When you hear it, you immediately think of the words, "Here comes the bride, all dressed in white," even though those lyrics were made up and added a hundred years later.

After Princess Victoria used this as her processional when she married Prince Frederick in 1858, it became all the rage—and is to this day the most used wedding processional.

I learned recently that the original sheet music, in Richard Wagner's own hand, was sold just a couple of years ago for 3.5 million dollars.

But then again, everything about weddings is expensive, right?

In fact, the wedding industry today is a multibillion-dollar-a-year business. I have read that the average wedding today is costing couples, and/or their parents, anywhere from $20,000 to $70,000 when all the expenses—the dinners, the travel, the printed materials, the rentals, the photographs, the reception, and, of course, the wedding gown—are included.

Everyone wants the perfect wedding. And there's nothing wrong with wanting an incredibly beautiful wedding, unless you're the father of the bride, to whom a backyard wedding and a cookout sounds really good.

But why not shoot for perfection!

You want the perfect beginning for those two people who walk into that ceremony single and in a matter of twenty minutes are going to leave married. Married, yes, but not yet grasping all the implications and responsibilities of marriage.

And every married couple knows it isn't long after that ceremony that the reality of marriage hits and the work begins.

Paul David Tripp in his book for couples entitled *What Did You Expect?* compares a wedding to a vacation brochure. He writes, "Unrealistic expectations always lead to disappointment. You know this is true if you've ever looked at a vacation Web site before traveling there. No vacation site will ever look as nice and function as well as it does on its promotional site on the Internet. . . . We took our family on a vacation to Disney World. We looked at that beautiful Disney literature. But we weren't told that we would stand under a blazing sun for 90 minutes in 120-degree heat and 200-percent humidity to ride a ride that takes 33 seconds."[1]

The truth is, when you stood and repeated those vows "for richer or for poorer," you had no idea how poor it would be. And when you promised "for better or for worse," you had no idea how worse it could get.

I love the humorous, tongue-in-cheek story I read some time ago. Three months after her wedding day, the young bride rushed into the pastor's office, hysterical. She said, "Pastor, my husband and I had our first big fight together, and it was really bad. It was just awful. Now what am I going to do?" The pastor said, "Just calm down. This isn't as bad as you think; every marriage has to have its first big argument. It's okay." She replied, "Well, okay, but what am I going do with the body?"

Maybe there are reasons why our world has grown skeptical of making the kind of commitment marriage demands. Maybe there's a reason you can now lease wedding rings a month at a time. Maybe there's a reason the traditional vow, "as long as life shall last," has been rewritten to say, "as long as love shall last."

In 1960, 70 percent of all adults were married; today, that number has dropped in half.[2] Now, more and more couples are cohabitating rather than marrying.

I think the situation was summarized quite well by an unbelieving actress, who was interviewed recently, shortly after separating from her second husband. She made this telling statement: "I think the idea of marriage is romantic; it's a beautiful idea." But then she said, "I don't think it's natural to be a monogamous person . . . It's a lot of work."[3]

In other words, because marriage is so much work, she has concluded that commitment to one person—through a monogamous marriage covenant—is unnatural.

And in a very real way, she's put her finger on the issue, even though, tragically, she doesn't know the solution. It's true that marriage cannot naturally become what God wants it to become; it requires spiritual wisdom; spiritual commitment, and a spiritual motivation.

The Bible says, "By wisdom a house is built, and by understanding it is established; and by knowledge the rooms are filled with all precious and pleasant riches" (Proverbs 24:3-4).

That's quite a promise: by God's wisdom a home—a marriage—is built; it is established, and it is filled with precious things.

So where can we find the wisdom of God that can build and establish and fill a marriage and a home with the right things?

Let's turn to the third chapter of the first letter from the apostle Peter.

THE SUBMISSION OF THE WIFE

In the same way, you wives, be submissive to your own husbands so that even if any of them are disobedient to the word, they may be won without a word by the behavior of their wives, as they observe your chaste and respectful behavior. (1 Peter 3:1-2)

In this chapter, we are going to focus on just the first phrase here: **In the same way, you wives, be submissive to your own husbands.**

In the same way makes us immediately ask the question, "In the same way as what?" The immediate context a few verses earlier points us to God the Son faithfully submitting Himself to the will of God the Father in the plan and purpose of redemption.[4]

We are to submit to God's purposes as did the Lord Jesus Christ. He is our supreme example in submission and humility.

The larger context begins in verse 13 of 1 Peter 2, which commands believers to submit to government institutions and authorities, even when they are ungodly, for they are ordained by God.

Then later, in verse 18, this verb *submit* takes us into the world of domestic servants, where servants are told to be submissive to their masters. The application in our day can properly be made to the employee/employer relationship.

Now in chapter 3 Peter writes, **In the same way, you wives be submissive to your own husbands.**

We must be careful here, though. Following orders and decrees and codes is right and proper for citizens, employees, and wives, but Peter isn't saying that mere outward submission alone will lead to the kind of marriage that fills its rooms with precious and pleasant riches.

This opening adverb, translated **in the same way**, means that the citizen and the employee and the wife—like God the Son—are to submit with the same sacred motive and with the same sacred perspective.[5]

They are ultimately submitting **in the same way**; that is, out of love for and obedience to God and for the exaltation of the glory of God and His wise purposes and plans, even if we do not fully understand them.

So, you could write in the margin above this phrase in verse 1 these words: "for the glory of God." **In the same way, you wives** *for the glory of God* **be submissive to your own husbands.**

Now if you have already skipped ahead in this chapter, you might have noticed that there are six verses dealing with wives and only one verse dealing with husbands.

That seems rather lopsided—*six times more* information given to wives than husbands. Some men might be tempted to say that's because they don't need as much instruction. But on the other hand, some women might argue it's because women love information more than men. After all, they actually read the directions whereas men don't.

All jokes aside, I agree with those who suggest that more space is devoted to Christian wives here simply because many of them had husbands who were either indifferent to or opposed to Christianity.

That definitely fits the context here, which speaks of submitting to husbands, some of whom may be **disobedient to the word.**

Over my years of ministry, I can say it's easily six times more likely for a devoted Christian wife to be suffering from an unspiritually minded husband than the other way around.

I think that was exactly the problem in Rome, where Peter was, and throughout the Roman Empire, and it is the problem today in America. Women want to know how to respond—how to submit to and respect their husbands— when they're in this most difficult situation of having husbands who aren't interested in the Word of God.

One author noted that no specific group of members in the church was more in need of warm encouragement, wise spiritual counsel, and understanding than these wives, many of whom were now married to unbelievers. And for a Christian wife in first-century Rome to abandon the pagan religion and lifestyle of her husband was to invite acute problems.[6]

Now, while Peter is speaking to all wives in every marriage, he's reminding these wives especially that the creation model of headship and submission applies to them too. In fact, it was more important than ever if their husbands were not responsive to the gospel.

Notice verse 1 again: **You wives, be submissive to your own husbands so that even if any of them are disobedient to the word, they may be won without a word.**

We will look at that "wordless testimony" more in the next chapter. For now, we want to examine exactly what it means for a wife to be submissive.

Just mention the word *submission*, and many women in our culture, and even in the evangelical church today, bristle with suspicion and even anger. Submission is probably one of the most controversial practical subjects in the New Testament.

WHAT SUBMISSION IS NOT

First, we need to understand what submission is *not*.

Submission is not an idea based on the belief that women are inferior morally, intellectually, emotionally, or spiritually.

Furthermore, submission is not blind obedience whereby the wife becomes a doormat for the man to walk over and she isn't allowed to make any decisions or suggestions or exercise any management responsibilities.

That may be how other religions in the world treat women, but that isn't Christianity.

In fact, as we will see later, men who misuse their authority and treat their wives callously or unkindly are told they might as well stop praying because God is not listening (1 Peter 3:7).

Further, biblical submission is not the basis for subjugation, or verbal or physical abuse. In fact, any Christian woman who is suffering physical abuse should call the police and then seek help and provision and counsel from godly shepherds for both her and her husband.

Submission is not a free pass for violence or even bad behavior. Warren Wiersbe said it this way: "Headship is not dictatorship, but the loving exercise of divine authority under the Lordship of Jesus Christ."[7]

Some suggest that submission and headship are the result of the fall of Adam and Eve and were never God's original design. But the truth is exactly the opposite. Adam and Eve were created with the inherent roles and responsibilities of headship and submission, respectively.

And they exhibited perfect unity, transparency, and cooperation.

Sin involved the violation of the principle of submission, for Eve acted on her own authority in response to Satan's offer, and then Adam violated the principle of headship by submitting to Eve's offer.

Following the fall of Adam and Eve, God delivered the effects of the curse to them in Genesis 3. The man would now work by the sweat of his brow, and the woman's desire would be for her husband, which literally means her desire would be to dominate and control her husband (See Genesis 3:16 along with 4:7).

So, the battle of the sexes, and the battle within marriage, came as a result of sin. Cooperation turned into competition. Wedlock turned into deadlock.

John Piper put it well when he said, "When sin entered the world, it ruined the harmony of marriage, not because it brought headship and submission into existence, but because it twisted them; it twisted man's humble, loving headship into hostile domination or lazy indifference. And it twisted woman's intelligent, willing submission into manipulative deference or brazen insubordination. Sin didn't create headship and submission; it ruined them and distorted them and made them ugly and destructive."[8]

So, what the Holy Spirit through Peter is beginning to explain to us in this paragraph is nothing less than a radical reversal of the effects of the curse pronounced in Genesis 3—a return to the kind of relationship God intended from the beginning for a husband and his wife.

WHAT SUBMISSION IS

So, what *is* biblical submission?

The Greek verb Peter uses here is *hupotasso*, which means to willingly rank under.[9] It's an administrative term that means to voluntarily assist in order to complete.

The late Donald Grey Barnhouse, a pastor and theologian, pointed out that in both the Greek and Latin languages, the word carries with it the idea of providing a foundation or personal assistance as a helper fit for the husband. Therefore, a woman with this God-glorifying perspective can say, "As I voluntarily submit to my husband, I am completing him. I am helping him fulfill his responsibilities, and I am helping him become the man, the husband, the leader God intended him to be."[10]

And how do we know Donald Grey Barnhouse made the right observation?

We know because that observation fits perfectly with God's creation design, revealed to us in Genesis 2:18, where God made that rather startling statement: "It is not good."

That was the first time in the early days of creation where something was categorized as "not good."

Everything God had created in Genesis 1 was summarized with the repeated statement, "And God saw that it was good . . . and God saw that it was good."

But now He says, "There's something that isn't good." He says further in verse 18, "It is not good for the man to be alone; I will make him a helper suitable for him."

So the concept of submission and assistance to the man existed in the Garden of Eden, long before sin occurred.

God said, "I'm going to make man a helpmeet, or helper suitable for him." In other words, "I'm going to create for Adam one who is a personal assistant in every way." The implication is that Adam would then be able to accomplish God's purposes for his life, which he would not have been able to accomplish without her assistance.

That doesn't mean single men, or women for that matter, can't complete God's assignment for their lives. This is simply God's creative design in general for those who marry. And for those who do marry—the ones Peter is addressing here—one of the defining roles of the helpmeet is that of assistant.

Let me illustrate this concept with a personal analogy. Perhaps you have an administrative assistant at work or an assistant in the shop or in the store or in the office. Is that person less valuable as a person than you? Are you superior to your assistant as an individual because you have more responsibility? Are you better because you make more money? Is your helper inferior to you in character and essence because he or she assists you? Are you closer to God because you're the administrator and this person is your assistant? To all these questions we must answer, "Of course not!"

So likewise, the husband isn't superior or better or more valuable or closer to God or more important to God's purposes and plans than is his helper.

And by the way, is that assistant at work really helpful to you if he or she never offers any ideas, questions you, corrects you, improves what you're doing, suggests a different way of doing something, or reminds you of things you have forgotten?

Listen, if your assistant doesn't do any of those things, he or she probably isn't giving you any real, valuable assistance.

Likewise, the submissive wife who voluntarily ranks herself under and assists her husband will offer ideas, ask questions, make corrections and improvements, suggest options and other ideas, and remind her husband of things he needs to do or forgot to do.

The world's idea of submission is very different from the biblical concept presented by the apostle Peter.

The world sees submission as:

- Second-class
- Inferior
- No initiative
- No backbone
- Unassertive
- Cowering
- Nonresistant
- Compliant

Scripture sees submission as:

- Loyalty
- Helpfulness
- Faithfulness
- Adaptability

- Deferential
- Completing
- Assisting[11]

In short, biblical submission is voluntary selflessness.[12]

Submitting to a husband's leadership is a choice of the wife to complement him with her unique gifts and talents rather than compete with him.

Biblical submission is the divine calling of a wife to honor and affirm her husband's leadership and help carry it through according to her gifts.[13]

In other words, wives, the principle and beauty of biblical submission is rooted in the creative act of God. He knew what your husband would need and thus, as with Eve, the first wife, God created *you* with your unique gifts and talents to complete him, which means that *together* you make a complete package.

Haven't you wondered why God puts opposites together? Why are two people who are so different brought together by the wise direction of God's Spirit?

Interestingly, those differences happen to be one of the most irritating things about marriage and at the same time one of the most enduring, protecting, balancing aspects of marriage.

I'll never forget a man telling me after church one day how different he and his wife were in every possible way. He'd been married for more than fifty years, and still, he said, they were so very different. This wise, older, godly man looked at me and laughed as he said, "The only thing my wife and I have in common is that we were both married on the same day."

That's it.

IMPORTANT REMINDERS

Before we wrap up this chapter, which in many ways is simply an introduction to a very broad subject, let me provide you with three general reminders.

Remember That You Are Building Your Marriage in a Fallen World

In a very real way, you're trying to build your marriage in a culture that is constantly trying to steal your tools.

You're busy trying to build something while people around you keep trying to take your pliers, hammer, screwdriver, wood glue, nails, and whatever else you have in your toolbox you're trying to use to build your marriage.

The world system is a gravitational pull away from selflessness and back into selfishness.

William Barclay wrote that submission is when a woman voluntarily chooses selflessness; it is the death of pride.[14]

And the world is constantly sending you messages: "What? That isn't going to be good for you. You won't be fulfilled that way!"

Yes, you will. The happiest, most fulfilling moments of life are selfless moments when pride is crushed and humility rises to serve someone else.

Jesus Christ, the most fulfilled person to ever walk on the planet, humbled Himself and took on the role of a servant (Philippians 2).

Remember That You Committed Yourself in Marriage to a Fallen Sinner

You happened to have married a sinner, and you are a sinner too! Indeed, marriage is the union of sinners. And what do sinners do?

One author wrote, "Sin turns us in on ourselves. Sin makes us shrink our lives to the narrow confines of our little self-defined world. Sin causes us to shrink our focus, motivation, and concern to the size of our own wants, needs, and feelings. Sin causes us to be way too self-aware and self-important. Sin causes us to be offended most by offenses against us and to be concerned most for what concerns us. . . . sin is essentially antisocial. We don't really have time to love our spouse, in the purest sense of what that means, because we are too busy loving ourselves."[15]

That's what sinners do.

As he begins to address the topic of marriage in chapter 3, Peter implies that marriage is not an escape from sinners. Rather, it is a means to glorify God by demonstrating the gospel to them, just as Christ loved us and died for us "while we were yet sinners" (Romans 5:8).

Remember That a Fallen Spouse Is God's Assignment for Developing Grace

When your ears hear and your eyes see the sin in your spouse, it is never an accident. Rather, in the plan and purpose of God, it is an opportunity for Him to demonstrate through you, loving confrontation and the transforming work of grace—the sharpening of iron against iron. These are the moments, one author wrote, when marriage becomes ministry.[16]

Who ever thought that your marriage would become a ministry? And ministry is hard work, right?

Ladies, before you were married you were looking for someone "just right" to marry. You were looking for Mr. Right. And then you found him. But after marriage you discovered that he isn't always Mr. Right. In fact, you soon began to wonder if you married Mr. Wrong.

The truth is, in a sense, we always marry the wrong person. And if we're honest, marriage shows us that we're the wrong person too. In fact, marriage is the great revealer of how wrong we are, on so many levels! It shows us how different we really are from the people we thought we were during courtship.

One of the first challenges of marriage is learning to love the stranger to whom you find yourself married.[17]

But this is nothing less than God's plan to work in us and through us to develop and demonstrate grace.

Paul David Tripp reminds us that the flaws we see in our spouse are not accidents but are the tools God uses to pry us out of the worship of self and into the worship of God.[18]

First, remember you are building your marriage in a fallen world. There are times in marriage when you are going to feel like you are riding a bicycle in the sand, but just keep pedaling.

Second, remember you are committed in marriage to a fallen sinner. Marriage is God's intentional plan for uniting two sinners and making them followers of Christ.

Third, remember a fallen spouse is God's assignment for developing and demonstrating grace.

And it begins in 1 Peter 3 with a wife submitting to a sinner and in so doing, demonstrating the ministry of marriage and the grace of God.

Chapter 2

WITNESSING WITHOUT WORDS

1 Peter 3:1b-2

While the Bible is our authoritative source of truth with regard to marriage, much of how we approach Scripture on the subject, unfortunately, is affected by the subtle and not-so-subtle influences of our culture.

A major shift has occurred in our culture over the past sixty years. In 1960, 878,000 unmarried people were living together. Today, that number has surpassed 10 million.

One Christian author stated that cohabitation is really a revelation of much broader shifts in our culture, such as an open attitude toward sexual activity. Added to this are the constant devaluation of marriage as an institution—as something too hard to be worth the effort—the fear of divorce, and our culture's complete abandonment of, or ignorance of, God's biblical plan.[1]

Today, the ever-present media, through print, television, mobile devices, and movies present one illustration after another of happy people cohabitating and one more marriage on the rocks.

One woman wrote, "I can't imagine getting hitched to anyone I hadn't taken on a test-spin as a roommate. Marriage before sharing a bathroom? Never!"[2]

In other words, if I still love him after cooking meals with him and cleaning the apartment with him and paying the bills with him and living with him, then it'll be a successful test-spin, and we'll get married.

You can expect that 10 million figure to be left in the dust over the next few decades, as many more couples decide to live together and presumably determine whether marriage with that person will work.

Of course, the problem with that decision-making process is so obvious that it gets missed in the discussion. You can't test-drive marriage. That is, you can't know what married life is like unless you're married.

Marriage is more than dishes and bills and cleaning and sharing a bathroom and a bedroom. It's a self-denying, self-sacrificing, self-encompassing commitment, and that commitment for life adds a dimension to the relationship that changes everything.

If someone slips up during a "test-drive," the test is over, and you're out the door. But a lifelong commitment to faithfully persevere through the ups and downs, through the thick and thin—for richer or for poorer, in sickness and in health, and for better or for worse—those vows can't be test-driven.

Marriage is not a month-to-month rental agreement.[3]

As one book puts it, "People are looking for something magical to happen in marriage. But magic doesn't make a marriage work; hard work does."[4]

The apostle Paul wisely exhorts believers, "Do not be conformed to this world, but be transformed by the renewing of your mind, so that you may prove what the will of God is" (Romans 12:2).

So, the ultimate question is not what your culture thinks marriage is, or what your own heart thinks it's supposed to be, or what you want it to be. The ultimate question is this: What is marriage and your role in it, according to the will of God, as revealed in the Word of God?

What is the will of God in this unique, lifelong, sanctifying relationship as you surrender to His design for marriage?

God's design involves the wife submitting to her husband like the church submits to Jesus Christ. That's no test run. The divine design also calls on the husband to love his wife just like Jesus Christ loves the church. That's not a test-drive either, especially when we consider that Jesus demonstrated His love by dying to redeem His bride (Ephesians 5:22-33).

There are incredibly challenging Creator-designed objectives for marriage.

And there are the added challenges we mentioned at the end of the last chapter: every marriage must be built in a fallen world; every marriage is between two fallen sinners; and fallen sinners represent God's assignment for developing and demonstrating patience and character and grace in our lives.

It is possible to live out the vows you made with joy and perseverance, if, and when, you depend upon the Spirit of God and pursue the will of God for marriage as revealed in the Word of God.

Now while every marriage requires spiritual power and personal commitment and not magic, Peter begins to focus his attention on what was—and is to this day—one of the most challenging marital relationships on the planet.

WHAT'S A WOMAN TO DO?

In the opening verse of 1 Peter 3, the apostle begins to provide warm encouragement and hope and instruction to a believing wife who happens to be married to a spiritually disinterested man . . . or, perhaps more specifically in this context, a spiritually *dead* man.

In the same way, you wives, be submissive to your own husbands so that even if any of them are disobedient to the word, they may be won without a word, by the behavior of their wives. (1 Peter 3:1)

As we saw in the first chapter, all wives are to be submissive to their husbands; that is, be willing assistants to their husbands in self-sacrifice and service. That's challenge enough. But in the second part of this verse, Peter zeroes in on wives who are married to men Peter describes as **disobedient to the word.**

Peter uses **the word** here as a technical term for the gospel.[5] The verb **disobedient** can be understood as meaning *unpersuaded*. So what is pictured in this case is someone who is unpersuaded as it relates to the gospel. In fact, the word carries the idea that he is deliberately and persistently unpersuaded.[6] He has clenched fists and a clamped jaw whenever you mention the gospel.

So Peter is personally addressing women in the church who were married to men who were openly opposed to Christianity. And the implication is that these wives were unbelievers when they married but now have become Christians.

Obviously, these women want to know what in the world a woman is supposed to do in a marriage like this. Her husband isn't just passively disinterested in the gospel but is now openly and stubbornly opposed to the gospel she has come to treasure and the living Lord she has come to know and follow.

Marriage for these women had become a spiritual one-way street.

This, by the way, can be the testimony of a woman married to a disobedient or disinterested believer, as well as one with a defiant, unbelieving husband. In either case, the principles are applicable.

So, Peter, what's the plan? What are these women to do?

Well, let me tell you first what Peter does not tell them to do.

THINGS TO AVOID

Leaving

First, Peter doesn't tell wives to leave their husbands at the first opportunity they get and start over.

They're new creatures in Christ, right? Should they start looking for a new marriage and a new husband as soon as possible? No. Instead, Peter tells them to go home to the husbands they have and, as we'll see, begin demonstrating the gospel to them.

The apostle Paul also spoke to wives with unbelieving husbands in his letter to the Corinthians:

> A woman who has an unbelieving husband, and he consents to live with her, she must not send her husband away. (1 Corinthians 7:13)

Paul adds in verse 14 that her unbelieving husband and children benefit from the holy influence of her life in the home. She may have no idea how impactful her life is for the gospel and will be for generations to come.

My great-grandmother had no idea what kind of legacy she was leaving her children and family by staying with her unbelieving husband and praying for his salvation for forty-two years.

And near the end of his life he came to Christ.

However, Paul does go on to say that if the unbelieving husband does not want to stay with his believing wife, she does not need to compel him to remain. Paul writes, "If the unbelieving one leaves, let him leave; the brother or the sister [that is, the believing spouse] is not under bondage in such cases" (1 Corinthians 7:15).

In other words, she is freed from the marriage vow her unbelieving husband no longer wants to maintain, and she is thus free to remarry.[7]

So, of course, the apostle Peter and the apostle Paul agree in their inspired instruction. And the first thing Peter emphasizes is that the believing wife doesn't have the right to divorce her husband at the first opportunity.

Preaching

Second, Peter does not tell wives to preach to their husbands at every opportunity.

By not demanding this of the wife, Peter is giving her hope. He's letting her know that she isn't responsible for convincing her husband that the gospel is true and that he's wrong and she's right.

Let's stop for a moment and try to appreciate how difficult marriage was for the wives Peter was addressing.

In the first-century Roman Empire—as in many countries to this day—the wife was expected to adopt her husband's religion.

There were many gods and goddesses and a plethora of temples. And the wife was expected to adopt her husband's patron god, who more than likely had been the patron god of his family for generations.

Now that she's a Christian, he's okay with her adding her God to his god and going along with the traditions of both.

But it isn't long before he realizes she isn't going to add her God to his god. In fact, the implication is that she's already tried to explain why she believes her God is the only God and every other god is a myth, and he is now totally against the gospel she's presented to him.

No doubt she has explained the exclusive claims of the gospel—that Jesus Christ is the way, the truth, and the life and that no one is going to the Father in heaven except through Him (John 14:6). She has let him know that she can't have dual allegiance; it isn't as simple as just worshipping at his temple and at her church.

As a result, her conversion has disrupted the family order and her husband's social order, which has no doubt upset him, not to mention the rest of the family.[8]

And so now, in Peter's context, the husband has become defiantly opposed to the gospel. The wife will naturally feel she hasn't done a good enough job convincing him, and so she is likely to conclude that what she needs to do is turn up the heat. Maybe he just hasn't heard the latest argument or read the latest book.

So what does she do? Put gospel tracts in his lunchbox? Set his car radio to Christian stations? Hang verses on the wall? Turn up the volume on the latest sermon from Ravi Zacharias?

In all seriousness, she is passionate about this. She knows he's going to hell, and she doesn't want him to go there!

So, she naturally thinks she needs to say more, not less!

But Peter says, "No, no. Say less." Note his words again: **they may be won without a word by the behavior of their wives.**

Notice too that Peter says **without a word.** He doesn't say, they may be won "without *the* word."[9] Indeed, "Faith comes from hearing, and hearing by the word of Christ" (Romans 10:17).

Of course she must be ready to speak about Christ; Peter isn't denying her that. But Peter is making sure she understands that taking the initiative isn't the solution; in fact, it may only deepen his defiance even more.

One author wrote on this text, "To persist in talking to someone who does not want to listen only hardens them more . . . but those whose hearts are hardened against preaching, may be softened by behavior."[10]

By the way, this truth applies to us all as we take the gospel to our world, making disciples. Remember this principle: No one has ever been argued into the kingdom of God.

No husband will ever say, "She finally wore me out and beat me down, and I went to church and got saved."

No one has ever been debated into the family of God.

So instead of turning up the heat, Peter tells wives to turn it down. "Let your witness be without words," you could render it—*without talking, without arguing.*[11]

Now granted, the wife's impatience is going to stem, not only from the reality of her husband's eternal destination, but also in part from the belief that if her husband gets saved, they will begin to experience marital bliss like they've never experienced.

After all, if he comes to faith, not only will he be saved, but he also can then save her from loneliness or frustration, right? Surely, such experiences are foreign to a Christian marriage! Surely, a Christian husband has a corner on communication skills.

Certainly marriage will be easy if you're married to a Christian, right? She will naturally think that. But married believers in the church, then and now, have discovered the rather disappointing truth that Christianity is not marital magic.

Christian marriages require work, and Christian marriages have communication difficulties because Christians are still fallen sinners.

I read a humorous story not long ago about a Christian couple who'd been married for sixty years. Throughout their lives they presented a model of unity and love to those around them and in their church. They had not kept any secrets from one another for all those years—except for a large box the wife kept on the top shelf of her closet.

When they got married, she put the box up there and asked her husband never to look inside it and never to ask questions about its contents. For sixty years the man honored his wife's request. In fact, he forgot about the box until his wife grew seriously ill, and the doctors said she wasn't going to recover.

So as this husband was putting his wife's things in order, he remembered that box in her closet, got it down, and brought it to her at the hospital. He asked her if perhaps now they might be able to open it together. She agreed. They opened the box, and inside were two pairs of crocheted mittens, along with a stack of five-dollar bills that totaled $45,000. The man was astonished.

The woman told her husband that the day before they were married, her grandmother told her that if she and her husband ever got into an argument with one another, they should work hard to resolve the matter. However, if her husband was unwilling to apologize about his part, she was to keep her mouth shut and crochet a pair of mittens.

The man was touched by this, because there were only two sets of mittens in the box. Sixty years—and only two times he'd been stubbornly unwilling to yield.

He was almost moved to tears. Almost! Then he asked her about the stack of money. "What's this?" His wife said, "Well, every time I crocheted a pair of mittens, I sold 'em for five dollars."[12]

If you're doing the math, that would be nine thousand stubborn moments.

Well, Peter has a Spirit-inspired strategy, and it doesn't have anything to do with crocheting mittens.

A HOPEFUL STRATEGY

Notice the end of verse 1 again: **they may be won without a word by the behavior of their wives.**

Earlier in 1 Peter 2:12, Peter used this same word for behavior when referring to the kind of life believers should live to silence the charges of unbelievers living around them.

He wrote, "Keep your behavior excellent . . . so that they may because of your good deeds, as they observe them, glorify God in the day of visitation."

And now Peter applies that same idea to wives married to unbelieving men, writing in verse 2, **as they observe your chaste and respectful behavior.**

So, just as the unbelieving world is watching Christians more than they even know (2:12), Peter implies that the unbelieving husband is watching his Christian wife more than she even knows.

That verb **observe** isn't referring to a casual glance or two. This verb refers to making careful observation.[13]

It's a rare verb that is most often used of a spectator.[14] The husband is carefully watching. He's an eyewitness.

In other words, Peter says to Christian wives, "Rather than hearing the gospel from you, your husbands are watching the gospel lived out in you, as eyewitnesses to your faith. Your demeanor and godly behavior are living out the undeniable, supernatural power of the gospel of Christ."

Peter offers the wife the possibility that her husband's defiant conscience may very well be softened over time, and he may be forced to admit the presence of a living God in her life. While he more than likely has mocked and ridiculed her faith, her translation of the gospel into life— right before her husband's eyes—may prove to be an irresistible witness.[15]

So, as they **observe your . . . behavior**, Peter now writes, make sure it is marked by two attributes.

Chaste Behavior

First, the wife's behavior must be **chaste.**

The word **chaste** can be translated pure. It has the idea of moral purity and a purity of conduct that is above innuendo or flirtation.

She should let him know by the way she acts around other men that she is committed to him alone.

I read recently of one pastor who at a wedding rehearsal was commenting on the symbolism of the unity candle, that candle that stands between the two candles that represent each family. He said, "After the middle candle is lit, blowing out the two side candles means the two—one from each family—have now become one." One member of the wedding party responded in surprise and all honesty, saying, "I always thought it meant that there were no other flames on the side."

That works too!

Respectful Behavior

Second, the wife's behavior must be **respectful.**

This **respectful behavior**—this respectful attitude toward him—is going to be a convicting testimony to him, simply because he will know in his heart that it is his wife who deserves such loyal respect far more than he does.

The wife ultimately is motivated to show whatever respect she can for her husband, not so much because he deserves it, but because by it she is showing respect and obedience and submission to God, whose will she is following and whose favor she is desiring above everything else.

And as a result of her behavior, she may get a new husband after all. Not another one but the same one—only new in Christ.[16]

Wouldn't that be something? Peter says it's possible.

Chuck Swindoll writes on this text, "This is the lifestyle of a wife, who with selfless cooperation and devotion to her husband, becomes a wife who is impossible to ignore.[17]

Let me encourage you wives; your children or grandchildren may become powerful allies in this household mission. They just might become powerful evangelists in the life of your husband.

One researcher illustrated the perception and impact of children by recounting the story of a three-year-old girl, who was raised in an atheistic family with no church contact and no Bible in the home. One day she asked her father, "Where did the world come from?" He answered her in naturalistic, evolutionary terms. Then he added, "Some people say that the world comes from a very powerful being, and they call him God." At this, the little girl started dancing around the room with joy, saying, "I knew what you told me wasn't true—it's him, it's him!"[18]

That must have made a lasting, profound impact upon her father.

Some Practical Suggestions

For the wife who wants to apply the instructions of the Holy Spirit given through the apostle Peter, what does this look like? What, specifically, can she do to demonstrate chaste and respectful behavior in her marriage?

Let me prime the pump with a few suggestions:

- Talk about him in a positive light to others.
- Don't slander him to others, or even speak negatively of him.
- Be warm and gracious to his family and friends— they're probably unsaved as well.
- Make your commitment to him obvious to those in his world.
- Ask him for his opinion and guidance whenever possible.
- Don't compliment other husbands to him; make your loyalty to him unconditional.
- Find areas where he is leading the way, and express appreciation.
- Make sure you're a good follower, even if you're a better decision maker.
- Don't expect perfection; make room for failure (it happens to non-Christian and Christian husbands alike).
- When asked about your faith, say as little as needed, not as much as possible.
- Expect God to work according to His timetable, knowing that a thousand years are, to Him, but one day.

- While God works His will throughout all eternity, focus on following His will for today, demonstrating the gospel to your husband through faithful, respectful love and service.

Probably the most famous example of a godly wife married to an unbeliever was Monica, the mother of Augustine. God used Monica in the conversion of both her son Augustine and her husband, late in life. Augustine became a significant theologian and church leader in the fourth century and is considered by many to be the theological forerunner of the Protestant Reformation.

Augustine wrote his autobiography in which he recounted the testimony of his mother, Monica, and her behavior to her unbelieving husband, who came to faith on his deathbed.

Augustine wrote of how his mother served her husband faithfully and diligently and sought to win him to Christ. She "preached" Christ to him by her behavior, and the Lord made her lovely to her husband. At last, when he was at the end of his earthly life, she won him to Christ.[19]

It doesn't take much for us to imagine the challenges Monica faced, the longing she felt, and the quiet prayers she offered as she looked for strength to go on in her quiet service for the glory of God.

I have little doubt that one passage in the New Testament that would have been especially precious to her, as it just might be for some readers today, is this one:

Wives, be submissive to your own husbands so that even if any of them are disobedient to the word, they may be won without a word by the behavior of their wives, as they observe your chaste and respectful behavior.

Chapter 3

MORE THAN SKIN DEEP

1 Peter 3:3-4

If you were to travel back to the first century, it might surprise you to find the Roman Empire to be absolutely enamored with clothing, jewelry, hairstyles, and physical strength and appeal, along with the latest in fashion.

One first-century historian wrote that in the empire there were as many hairstyles as there were honeybees. Hair was waved, curled, dyed—sometimes jet black, sometimes auburn. Wigs were imported from Germany and as far away as India, and the most popular wigs were blonde. Added to the hair were hair bands, pins, and combs made of ivory and tortoiseshell; and for the wealthy, combs were crafted in gold and studded with gems.

When the apostles were living and writing their letters to the New Testament churches, silks, pearls, perfumes, and jewelry imported from India alone amounted to what would be $2 billion annually in today's economy.

I discovered in my studies that purple was the favorite color in the early centuries because it was the most expensive cloth; one purple garment would cost as much as the average person's annual salary.

If you could afford them, diamonds, emeralds, and opals were favorite gems; one Roman woman had a ring valued at $2 million.

Pearls were coveted the most. Nero, the emperor, had a room in his palace where pearls were used as wallpaper (just to demonstrate that he had more pearls than anybody else). And the historian Pliny wrote that the wife of the emperor Caligula once appeared in a gown covered with pearls and emeralds, at a cost, today, of $20 million.[1]

America didn't invent glamor and glitz. In fact, early Christianity was growing in a luxuriant and decadent world of glamor and glitz, a world obsessed with physical appearance.

Women in the first century had an array of highly developed cosmetics imported from around the world. They had rouge for their cheeks and lipstick in a variety of colors, as well as eyeliners in colors that included brown, black, and green; they had fingernail polish in colors that included yellow and orange.

One author wrote that because of this obsession throughout the Roman Empire, women were under enormous pressure to look beautiful and fashionable.[2]

I can't help but think that the first century and the twenty-first century have a lot in common.

I did some research and found that Americans now spend $40 billion annually on cosmetics alone. That's a lot of lipstick in a lot of colors!

Men are involved in this too. In fact, altogether, Americans shelled out $1.4 billion in one year just for over-the-counter teeth whiteners . . . $1.4 billion!

In terms of cosmetic sales worldwide, the country of Japan comes in second to America, with an annual expenditure of $26 billion for cosmetics.

And these figures do not include money spent on cosmetic surgeries, which bring in another $10 billion a year plus.

The truth, however, is that none of this brings a sense of contentment. In fact, although the United States is first in cosmetics spending, global surveys place the country at number 23 in the "satisfied with life" category. And Japan is second in spending on cosmetics but ranks number 90 in life satisfaction.[3]

But the obsession is only moving faster and deeper—and more dangerous and invasive.

In an article for the *Smithsonian Magazine* a few years ago, the author catalogued forms of cosmetic surgeries that are growing more and more mainstream.

For instance, in New York, women are having their toes surgically shortened and then strengthened with metal pins so they can fit into three-inch Jimmy Choo stiletto heels. I don't know who Jimmy Choo is, but he's not worth that surgery.

In China, where beauty pageants were once outlawed and considered "spiritual pollution," they are now being held around the country. And since taller women are considered more beautiful, a procedure is becoming popular whereby shinbones are severed and metal inserts are implanted so that three inches of new bone can be grown. It's an operation filled with risks of deformation and weakened muscles—but you gain three inches in height.

This author concludes, "[There is a] global quest for bodily perfection . . . and it has generated an almost pathological obsession with our bodies."[4]

I can't help but think of the apostle Paul when he wrote that the unbelieving world is marked by worshipping what he calls, their belly. He writes, "Their god is their belly" (Philippians 3:19 ESV). In other words, whatever it is they physically desire—whatever they want for their body—they pursue.

Now the Bible never endorses a disregard for a healthy body. It never encourages misusing or mistreating the body. It doesn't tell us the body doesn't matter so we can ignore what it truly needs. But Paul strikes a needed balance by writing to Timothy, "Bodily discipline is only of little profit, but godliness is profitable for all things, since it holds promise for the present life and also for the life to come" (1 Timothy 4:8).

Paul makes it clear that while physical exercise has some value, it's just not as important as spiritual exercise. So Paul warns us not to lose sight of the fact that our bodies aren't the priority, and the obvious reason he implies is that they aren't permanent—in fact, God has new, glorified bodies planned for us in the life to come, bodies that will literally last forever.

In the meantime, we Christians struggle with balancing physical appearance and spiritual development. We all have the desire to look as good as we can, but the potential for obsession—and imbalance—didn't automatically go away when we became Christians. Unbelievers aren't the only ones who struggle with the way they look.

The apostle Peter is about to challenge us all with the truth that demonstrating the uniqueness of the gospel means living lives that are not preoccupied with physical appearance.

EXTERNAL ADORNMENT

In the first verses of 1 Peter 3, the apostle is writing to wives; he's writing to converted women in the early church, many of them newly converted, no doubt, and they are married to unbelieving husbands. These are women who've come out of a culture I've just described, a culture that worshipped youth and physical strength, a culture that worshipped the body. Just go to a museum and look at the statues excavated from earlier centuries—it was all about the perfect body. It was out of that decadent world of fashion and obsession with physical perfection that these Christian women were saved.

Listen to what the Spirit of God through Peter has to say to these women.

Your adornment must not be merely external— braiding the hair, and wearing gold jewelry, or putting on dresses; but let it be the hidden person of the heart, with the imperishable quality of a

gentle and quiet spirit, which is precious in the sight of God.

Peter is delivering life-changing truth that can free women (single or married, young or old)—and men too, by application—from focusing their lives on their appearance.

Peter begins by saying, in essence, "Let me challenge you regarding your **adornment**." The word he uses for **adornment** is *kosmos*, which gives us our English words cosmos (the ordered universe) and *cosmetics* (the ordering of the face). Peter highlights three cosmetic activities: braiding the hair, wearing jewelry, and putting on dresses.

Now we must be careful here. Peter isn't forbidding anything; he's just prioritizing things.

There are people who have concluded from this text that a woman should not let her hair down in public—either braided or loose—and they take their cue from this text. Others take this text to mean a woman should not wear jewelry in public either.

I was talking to my older brother recently about this text, and he told me of a ministry trip he took to Romania in the early 1990s. The churches there were embroiled in debate over whether a woman should wear a wedding band in public—and this text was at the heart of the debate. Many were arguing that Peter was forbidding any kind of jewelry and that wedding bands were jewelry and thus forbidden.

Churches were literally splitting over the interpretation and application of this passage.

Well, if we apply this verse consistently, we would have to conclude that if Peter is forbidding a woman from braiding her hair and wearing jewelry, he's also forbidding her from wearing a dress—and I doubt he's doing that.

The original word Peter uses here for braiding occurs in the New Testament only here. It's not a reference to a hairstyle as much as it is to the time and activity of braiding.

This wasn't a couple of pigtails and you're out the door. The braiding Peter refers to took hours of time and attention, and in his day it had become a public display of wealth and leisure. It set you apart.

Again, Peter doesn't forbid it. He's not concerned with pigtails; he's concerned with priorities.

The verb Peter uses in the phrase **wearing gold jewelry** is another word found only here in the New Testament. It can be translated "putting around."

This wasn't just a matter of wearing a gold ring; this, again, involved an ostentatious display of wealth.

Isaiah provides a rare look into the use of jewelry and other ornaments in his day when he wrote about the practice of women wearing expensive bells on their sandals, jewelry around their ankles, multiple bracelets on their wrists and upper arms and necks, finger rings, nose rings, and dangling earrings (Isaiah 3). You didn't just see these women coming; you heard them coming a mile away.

Isaiah's description, and Peter's description as well, is of a woman who loads on the jewelry and gets the desired attention, not because of who she is, but because of what she owns and how she looks.

The jewelry might change through the centuries, but the principle warning remains the same: Women, be careful what you wear. Be careful how you get attention. Be careful what you are communicating by what you wear. Don't wear your wealth on your sleeve. Don't show off, especially in the church. And outside the church assembly, don't demonstrate that your priorities are focused on the physical.

The third adornment mentioned by Peter at the end of verse 3 is **putting on dresses.** This doesn't mean a woman can't wear a beautiful dress. That's not his point.

Peter is referring to the wearing of extravagant clothing for the sake of showing off. And in this context, it carries the idea of gaining attention for all the wrong reasons.

Peter certainly isn't telling Christian women to look unkempt or unattractive. He isn't even forbidding braided hair, jewelry, and nice clothes, just the excessive focus on such externals. The apostle is now ready to redefine what is truly beautiful—what is really worthy of attention. And such beauty is more than skin deep!

INTERNAL ADORNMENT

Having said what not to focus on, Peter moves on to tell women where to put their time and energy.

But let it be the hidden person of the heart. (1 Peter 3:4)

Stop for a moment.

The Greek word for **heart** here is *kardia*. In biblical terms, the heart is the center of who we really are. This immaterial part of us defines who we are. It is the center of our thoughts, motives, and choices. As a man thinks in his heart, so is he (Proverbs 23:7).

For the believer, the heart is equivalent to the regenerated nature. As one author notes, this is the place where the Holy Spirit's inner work of grace is accomplished "and true beauty becomes real and long-lasting."[5]

So, Peter is contrasting the physical world, the *kosmos*, with the spiritual world, the *kardia*; that is, the public world and the private heart. He's telling women to focus on their heart—to spend more time grooming their hearts spiritually than grooming their hair and dressing their bodies physically.[6]

Spiritual Qualities

. . . with the imperishable quality of a gentle and quiet spirit. (1 Peter 3:4)

And just what should they be developing in the privacy of their hearts? Peter gives us two qualities: **a gentle and quiet spirit.**

The word for **gentle** means gracious or considerate. Being gentle is showing kindness as opposed to being pushy and demanding.

Gentleness, of course, is found in the list of the fruit of the Spirit in Galatians 5, which means this isn't for women only but for men as well.

Sometimes the word for **gentle** is translated "meek" in the New Testament. It's used to describe Jesus Christ in Matthew 11:29. Meekness doesn't mean weakness; it's power under control, emotion under control.

So, Peter isn't recommending that women become doormats, or open themselves to abuse. He isn't suggesting that women can't share their minds or their opinions.[7]

In fact, Jesus was known by this same quality. He was gentle, or meek, and He definitely spoke His mind and shared His opinion. But the Lord was never out of control. He was always intentional and purposeful.

The second quality for internal development is a **quiet spirit**. This doesn't mean she never makes a sound; the word Peter uses here relates to peace. She's literally at peace. This is a spirit that calmly bears the disturbances created by others without creating a disturbance itself.[8]

When you think about the immediate context, this inner quality is critical—and absolutely dependent upon the Holy Spirit.

Here's a believing wife, married to an obstinate man who cares nothing for the gospel and wants nothing to do with it. Yet in the midst of this turmoil, she has a sense of internal peace. Things around her are warlike, and she's pursuing peace.[9]

This is the undeniable work of God. It is so unusual that her unbelieving husband won't be able to ignore that there is something different about her.

For the woman who wants to demonstrate the power of the gospel to her disbelieving or disobedient husband, Peter says these are the qualities that are impossible to ignore: gentleness and quietness.

The truth is, an unbelieving husband won't take note of how many times his Christian wife prays, how many chapters of the Bible she reads, or how often she goes to church. But he will notice her demeanor, not only as she goes about the routine duties of life, but also as she faces turmoil and difficulties.

This is attention-grabbing—and for the right reason. This is different. This is beautiful.

A popular proverb puts it this way: "A woman whose smile is wide and whose expression is glad has a kind of beauty no matter what she wears."

This beauty is more than skin deep.

Peter reminds these wives, and every woman in the body of Christ, of truth they won't get from television or a magazine or from Madison Avenue. The true essence of feminine beauty is not outward adornment but inward attitudes that express themselves with kindness and confidence.[10]

You can't buy these qualities of beauty. They aren't sold over the counter; you can't find them on sale. In fact, they can't be purchased at all; they are developed by the Spirit of God, down deep—below the skin, inside the hidden person of the heart.

Unique Qualities

These two qualities of gentleness and quietness are unique for two reasons.

First, notice earlier in verse 4, Peter writes that these qualities are **imperishable.**

That's another way of saying – these qualities will never go out of style.[11] What's in fashion will eventually go out of fashion, but these never will! They are **imperishable.**

In simple terms, this is stuff that lasts. The word translated **imperishable** literally means *unfading*.[12] Peter is telling women of all ages, here is a beauty that will never fade away.

Everything about us is getting older, even if we try to deny it. No matter how young we still see ourselves, the temporary beauty of youth is fading away.

Someone sent me this story in an email some time ago. A woman was sitting, waiting for her first appointment with a new dentist. She noticed his DDS diploma, which bore his full name. Suddenly, she remembered that a tall, handsome, dark-haired young man with the same name had been in her high school class many years ago. She wondered, *Could this dentist be the same guy I had a crush on way back then?*

She quickly discarded any such thought when he came into the room; he was slightly bent over; a balding, gray-haired man with deep wrinkles in his face. *He's way too old to have been my classmate, she thought.*

Still, after he examined her teeth, she asked, "Did you happen to attend Morgan Park High School?"

"Yes! And I'm still a Morgan Mustang," he said with school pride.

"Well," she asked, "when did you graduate?"

He replied, "In 1959 . . . why do you ask?"

She said, "I knew you looked familiar. You were in my class!"

"Really?" he said, looking at her closely. "What class did you teach?"

Again, Peter is telling his readers, "Don't focus on something that's fading away, something that requires more and more cosmetics. Instead, focus on dressing your heart. Allow the inner working of the Spirit of God to produce character in you because character doesn't fade away. It's the stuff that lasts.

Second, we find in the last part of verse 4 that these qualities are not only **imperishable** but are also **precious in the sight of God.**

This word for **precious** doesn't mean, "Well, isn't that sweet." No, this is a word that means valuable, costly, even priceless.

Again, this is a play on words. While the world lavishes money on things that have high price tags, God informs us that the most valuable things in life are not in our wardrobe; they're in our hearts. It is upon a gentle/gracious and quiet/calm spirit that God has stamped the highest price tag.

Peter's words here are directed to women, but there is something for men to learn as well. Christian men need to make sure they're modeling the heart of God by placing less value and attention on a woman's figure or face and more value on her faith and her faithfulness to Christ and His church.

It would be an immense help to Christian women if the men in our congregations clearly rejected the world's obsession with the body. That obsession has come at a terrible cost for women—the sense of never looking good enough; never being pretty enough; never measuring up; feeling inferior, ugly, and unlovable. Christian men must be careful not to imitate the world's value system by encouraging women to focus on the wrong things.

OBSERVATIONS

We can summarize what Peter is saying to wives and to women in general with three observations.

1. *What matters most about you will never be hanging in your closet or tucked away in a jewelry box.*

In other words, what matters most has nothing to do with style—it has everything to do with your spirit.

It has nothing to do with less wrinkles or newer clothes or shinier jewelry. That stuff isn't eternally valuable. What the Spirit of God is developing as spiritual fruit is priceless.

2. *What impacts your husband—and the rest of the world for that matter—and brings God great glory isn't your appearance but your attitude.*

Peter is talking specifically about graciousness and calmness.

3. *What the world pursues with great obsession is temporary; what the Christian pursues with great passion is eternal.*

Perhaps you've noticed your natural inclination to size people up when you first meet them at the job or in the classroom. You take an immediate physical inventory. It's unconscious—you don't make it obvious—but you take note of their face, their accent, their clothing, maybe even their shoes.

It starts at a young age. I've talked to teachers of elementary students who have told me that by the first grade everybody is rated by what they wear and what they own and how they talk. In fact, if you don't have a smartphone by the third grade, you're obviously a nobody.

This is the world's way of sizing people up! This is the old way of thinking, and as Christians we must grow out of it.

Have you noticed that after you get to really know someone—no matter what that earlier mental inventory was—those physical things, those external attributes, don't register as important anymore?

After you get to know people, you measure their value by their personality, their work ethic, and their response to difficulties and pressures and hard work. You couldn't care less anymore what kind of shoes they're wearing or what kind of car they drive. Those things don't define who they really are.

You see, the world out there never gets past that initial inventory. It's still all about clothes and fashion and complexion and style. They never get past the temporary. They never get any farther than skin deep. To them, everything will always be about fashion and figure and face.

To God, what matters most is heart and character and spirit.

With that in mind, let all of us, men and women alike, look into the spiritual mirror today and think about this coming week.

How much time will you spend grooming your face compared to the time you'll spend grooming your faith?

How much effort will you give this week to working on external things compared to the effort you'll make working on internal things?

How much time will you spend exercising your body at the gym compared to the time you will spend exercising your spirit in God's Word?

Is there room left in your schedule to work on priceless things? Let me encourage you, as a believer, to plan for regular exercise in the Word this week. And make sure gentleness/graciousness and quietness/calmness are part of that internal workout that takes place down deep —much deeper than skin deep—down deep in your heart.

Chapter 4

DAUGHTERS OF SARAH

1 Peter 3:5-6

London-based luxury travel company is offering to plan your destination wedding—down to the last detail. In fact, the company guarantees that rain will not ruin your wedding day. Is this really possible? According to the company's website, the answer is "Absolutely, yes."

The site promises:

In order to ensure the most perfect of perfect days . . . we can now offer our customers a 'cloud-bursting' service that can 100% guarantee fair weather and clear skies for your wedding day! Currently available to customers organising a destination wedding in France . . . the service employs the talents of pilots and meteorologists and takes over three weeks to plan, and uses silver iodide to 'seed' the clouds—essentially giving the water vapor something to condense around to produce rain [so that by the time of your wedding, the skies are clear]. Costs start from £100,000 [about $132,000] . . . But then again, you can't put a price on perfection.[1]

Frankly, I doubt anyone has had the perfect wedding ceremony. I read recently of a couple who listed the wrong passage from the Bible in the wedding program. They caught the mistake in time, though. Had they not, a cousin would not have read a passage on the love of God but one on the Antichrist.

A pastor friend of mine told me about a wedding ceremony he performed in a small country church in the dead of winter. The heating system included those metal running boards along the sides of the church that clicked and popped with dry heat. Unfortunately, the janitor had waited too long to turn on the heat, so just before the guests began arriving, he went down into the basement and turned it up really high to try to warm the building quickly. Then he forgot about it and went home. By the time the ceremony began, the church was hot and stuffy. As a result, one bridesmaid fainted—and then another.

Finally, the bride herself fainted. They revived her, but moments later she fainted again. Someone gave her a towel soaked in cold water, and she spent the rest of the ceremony on the kneeling bench with the towel on her face. The couple had planned to race off on their honeymoon after the ceremony was over, but the bride refused to go. She simply couldn't remember saying any vows—in fact, she couldn't remember getting married at all. It was only after they hurriedly played a video of the ceremony for her in the pastor's office and she saw herself getting married that she agreed to leave.

Hopefully, the honeymoon went better than the wedding.

There's no such thing as a perfect wedding ceremony. And the truth is, even if you had a near-perfect wedding ceremony, it would soon be replaced by a not-so-perfect marriage. And that's because marriage is the union of two imperfect people. Marriage is two sinners uniting in covenant together before God.

From the first couple recorded in human history all the way to the twenty-first-century church, we're still in need of answers to the same basic questions about marriage. And the questions all revolve around the same issue: How is this thing supposed to work?

THE SUBMISSION OF HOLY WOMEN

In the opening comments of 1 Peter 3, the apostle addresses wives and focuses on the concept of submission. Peter then moves on to talk about the appearance, behavior, and internal attitudes of a godly wife. His comments relate specifically to Christian wives whose husbands are unbelievers, but these truths also apply to believing women in general.

Peter rejects contemporary thinking. He makes it clear that true beauty isn't defined by how many heads turn as you take a spin down the red carpet. True beauty isn't external but comes from the inside, and the wardrobe of genuine beauty is a "gentle and quiet spirit"; that is, graciousness and peace, or composure.

Peter has spent several verses on giving wives—and women in general—*instruction* and *motivation*. Now he gives an *illustration*.[2]

For in this way in former times the holy women also, who hoped in God, used to adorn themselves, being submissive to their own husbands. (1 Peter 3:5)

First, notice that Peter is circling back around to the issue of submission. He began in verse 1, saying, "In the same way, you wives, be submissive to your own husbands" Now he brings it up again at the end of this paragraph, speaking in verse 5 of wives **being submissive to their own husbands.**

Peter, we should remember, is a married man. Matthew 8:14-15 tells us the Lord Jesus healed Peter's mother-in-law, and you typically don't get a mother-in-law without getting the benefit of a wife.

So is this subject stuck on Peter's mind because he's having trouble with his wife? No. Under the inspiration of the Holy Spirit, he's simply presenting truths every generation needs. This is important instruction on how to leave the wedding ceremony and engage in married life.

The Nature of Submission

As we learned in our exposition of verse 1, the Greek word for **submissive** means to willingly rank under.[3] It can be expanded to mean voluntarily arrange and adapt and serve with deference and respect.[4] The word actually is an administrative term that carries the idea of voluntarily assisting in order to bring to completion.

God created the wife's role to serve as a divinely ordained assistant to her husband. In fact, God used that same language all the way back in the Garden of Eden as He was about to create Eve and walk her down the aisle to Adam: "I will make him a helper suitable for him" (Genesis 2:18). That's another way of saying, "The man really needs help!"

A wife who embraces this God-glorifying perspective understands that as she voluntarily submits to her husband, she is actually completing him. She is helping him fulfill his responsibilities, helping him become the man, the husband, and the leader God intended him to be.[5]

When you mention the idea of submission today, however, people immediately assume you came to America on the *Mayflower*. The idea of submission is archaic at best and tantamount to slavery at worst.

God calls it strength. As we learned in our last chapter, a submissive woman is a woman of power, a woman under control.

1. *Submitting to a person who has a position of authority doesn't mean one has less value.*

In fact, submission doesn't have anything to do with value but with structure and function in the home.

That policeman who stops me on the interstate for not reaching the minimum speed—happens to me all the time—has unique authority I don't have. And it has nothing to do with character or holiness or value. He simply occupies a role that is different from mine.

2. *Submission in marriage doesn't mean a wife is inferior to her husband.*

In fact, any man who thinks submission of a wife is based on the inferiority of women is revealing his own inferiority complex.

3. *Submission does not mean blind obedience.*

God's idea of a wife serving as her husband's helper means that she has things to contribute and improve and even correct, as we will see in a moment. Any man who believes submission is blind obedience is himself blind.

The Nature of Submissive Women

One of the great challenges for women hearing this letter read in the first-century assembly was that there weren't elective courses available on marriage and family. There was no Amazon.com with a quarter of a million books on marriage alone (not all of which get it right, of course). The church was young, and the New Testament itself was just then being written.

As we have noted, Peter's words here are directed specifically to women who are in very difficult marriages to unbelievers, men Peter describes in verse 1 as "disobedient to the word." The expression indicates unbelief, but perhaps it is broad enough to include men who claim to know Christ but live ungodly lives.

For believing women scattered throughout the Roman Empire, there were few resources to draw on, but Peter reminds them of one they would have known well—the Old Testament.

Observe again verse 5:

For in this way in former times, the holy women also, who hoped in God, used to adorn themselves, being submissive to their own husbands.

Peter is essentially telling them that submission isn't new, and, even more encouraging, these women aren't alone. In fact, he reminds them that believing women throughout the history of redemption were adorned by these same submissive qualities of graciousness and composure.

Notice in verse 5 the two descriptions of these women. First, they were **holy women**. The word *holy* means separated for God's glory. It doesn't mean they were perfect women, but it does mean they lived their lives for God's glory.

Second, **they hoped in God,** meaning they looked to God as their source of strength.[6] They looked to God for their provision and for their courage and purpose in life.

Their **hope**—that is, their settled conviction in God—wasn't determined by their culture or their peers or even their husbands. They were **holy women . . . who hoped in God.** These were women of old who lived their lives for God's glory, depending every day on God's power.

Their hope was *in God!* There is our rock. There is our fortress. He is our strong tower and safe refuge.

Peter tells the women he's writing to that these women in past centuries were known for their character and holiness and trust. They were not inferior intellectually or moral cowards.

Peter doesn't stop to list these Old Testament women of courage and character, but we can imagine many in the assembly as his letter was being read would have mentally wandered off into the corridors of Old Testament history and recalled some favorite names of holy women from the past.

Perhaps they would have thought of Abigail, the woman of composure and grace who was married to a foolish, arrogant farmer named Nabal.

When David and his troops were in hiding from King Saul, they graciously protected Nabal's flocks and herds from thieves and wild animals. But when David needed food and sent a message to Nabal asking for provisions, Nabal responded in arrogance. He mocked David and his men and refused to feed them. Consequently, David and his men set out to get revenge.

Abigail heard what was happening and took matters into her own hands to save her foolish husband's neck. She loaded up food and met David and his men before they reached the family estate. She wisely diffused the situation and saved her husband's life by giving David and his men the food and provisions they needed. David praised her wisdom and turned back.

Abigail returned home to a difficult marriage to a selfish and arrogant husband, but she didn't keep from her husband the truth of what had happened and how his foolish decision almost cost him his life. Early the next morning she told him that David and his men had planned to kill him because of his foolish decision.

We're not told how that conversation went or the tone of her voice. We can imagine, though, that the interaction wasn't very pleasant. Indeed, after she finished confronting him and telling him the truth, he had a heart attack and died.

The point isn't that she confronted him and he died. The point is, she did the right thing. She took the initiative and communicated grace and a warning to David and the truth to her husband. You can read the full account in 1 Samuel 25.

Peter assumed the early church knew the Old Testament narratives and left it to them to do their own study. The reason I think of Abigail is that her testimony of courage and faith certainly would resonate with the women Peter is addressing in this specific context—those who were married to unbelieving men.

Peter thus provides an illustration for the church. These women of old who were clothed with this kind of character and grace and strength and value were also clothed with submission to their own husbands. That is, they were dedicated to supporting and encouraging and helping their husbands.

THE SUBMISSION OF SARAH

Now Peter shifts his focus to one woman in particular. Look at verse 6:

. . . just as Sarah obeyed Abraham, calling him lord. (1 Peter 3:6)

That right there is a husband's favorite verse, isn't it? **Sarah obeyed Abraham, calling him lord.** That's a verse to write out on an index card and tape on the refrigerator.

But let's look closer. Peter is referring to that moment recorded in Genesis 18 when angelic visitors announced to the elderly Abraham that his wife, Sarah, was going to have a son within a year.

When she heard this announcement, Sarah laughed at such a thought, which was indeed rather ludicrous, given the fact that she was nearly ninety years old at the time and Abraham one hundred. The Bible records in Genesis 18:12 that Sarah laughed to herself, saying, "After I have become old, shall I have pleasure, my lord being old also?"

This is where Sarah referred to Abraham as her **lord**. Of course, people have jumped all over this expression, arguing that it proves the patriarchal concept of submission is tantamount to slavery.

But all you need to do is read what the Bible says about Abraham and Sarah and their marriage, and you'll discover that Sarah wasn't the household servant. She wasn't bowing and scraping. She wasn't a wallflower or weak minded, and she definitely wasn't a doormat.[7]

"My lord" was simply an expression of respect and one that Peter indicates Sarah commonly used. Peter uses a present tense participle when he says Sarah was **calling him lord**; in other words, this was an ongoing practice.[8]

There was a pattern of respect for her husband in Sarah's heart and life. She had an ongoing, undergirding attitude of deference and consideration and esteem toward Abraham.

In the ancient world—in fact, up until a few centuries ago—"my lord" was an expression one might use to show deference and courtesy. Keep in mind, of course, this is *lord* with a little *l*, not a capital *L*.

Sarah had the utmost respect for Abraham, but if you look closely at their marriage, you discover that more than once Sarah challenged her husband to think differently and act differently.

Maybe you've heard about the nervous young bride. On the day before her wedding, she went to speak with her minister. "I'm afraid I might not make it through the ceremony. I'm just so nervous I can hardly breathe!" she said.

The minister assured her everything would be fine. "Look," he said, "when you enter the church tomorrow and the processional begins, you will be walking down the same aisle you've walked many times before. So, concentrate on that aisle. Then, when you get halfway down the aisle, look up a bit, and you'll see the altar in the front, which you've seen a thousand times before; concentrate on that table—the cross sitting on top of it next to the Bible. And then when you're almost to the altar, you will see your groom, the man you love. Just concentrate on him." The bride was relieved with this advice and left to prepare for her big moment.

The next day, right on cue, as composed as ever, she walked down that aisle with confidence. Those who looked carefully, however, could see her lips moving, and the people closest to the aisle could hear her whispering to herself over and over again, "Aisle, altar, him. Aisle, altar, him."

Many wives are determined to "alter" their husbands. They see better than anyone his shortcomings, and they desire to see positive changes. Therein lies the challenge for any godly wife—how to challenge and rebuke her husband and encourage needed changes while showing him the greatest respect. She must learn to become an instrument in the hand of God to offer wise counsel without cutting her husband off at the knees or wounding his spirit. It is a balancing act that requires godly wisdom.

Sarah, of course, also created her own set of problems. Some of her advice was self-centered and not influenced by God's Spirit, and when this was combined with Abraham's lack of spiritual leadership at times, the couple ended up heading in the wrong direction.

The Spirit of God moved Peter to illustrate submission through the life of Sarah, not because Sarah was perfect, not because she had a perfect marriage, and not because she had a perfect husband; she was chosen despite all that. Sarah didn't live out perfection, but she pursued a pattern of submissive cooperation and assistance.

In fact, Sarah willingly followed her husband into unknown territory out of obedience to the call of God and the promise of a covenant fulfilled through their descendants. And going through all the challenges of where that narrative of faith would take them ultimately landed her in Hebrews 11 as one of the signature heroes of the faith.

And Peter writes that every wife who makes Sarah a spiritual mentor bears a family resemblance to this spiritual mother-figure. Notice the rest of verse 6:

. . . and you have become her children if you do what is right without being frightened by any fear.

The English translation makes it sound like you can earn your way into Sarah's family of faith. A better understanding of what Peter is saying is that you demonstrate that you have become Sarah's daughter when you do the right thing.

Note, finally, the last words of verse 6: **without being frightened by any fear.**

At times, it's a fearful thing for a woman to follow her husband's lead, knowing he can make mistakes. It is critical, therefore, that her hope—her confidence—ultimately is in the sovereignty of God, who watches over her.

The women Peter was writing to were harassed and intimidated by their unbelieving husbands, as well as by a culture that had little patience for the gospel. Peter is effectively saying that a woman must not allow the obstinacy of an unbelieving husband—or culture—to scare her out of her faith or intimidate her into denying her Savior.[9]

SUBMISSION APPLIED

So, how do we apply Peter's divinely inspired instruction? After all, you might be asking the question, "What do I do if I have an unsaved or spiritually disobedient husband?"

Let me offer four practical suggestions:

1. *First, find a godly woman who can become your mentor—a Sarah. If you're married to a husband who doesn't lead,*

love, and care for you, then you need a woman who can give you wise advice and help you entrust yourself to God so that you can stay balanced rather than grow bitter.

2. *Second, take a life inventory to see if God is communicating indirectly through your husband's attitudes and actions that there are things He wants to change in your heart and life. What action do you need to take?*

3. *Third, ask a very small circle of friends to pray for your husband. This isn't a time for saying, "Guess what my husband just did" but rather, "Pray for my husband to trust in Christ," or "Pray that he will begin to walk genuinely with Christ."*

4. *Fourth, stay committed in your own study of the Word and in your prayer life. Only the Spirit of God can comfort and heal and help you handle the pressures that are so overwhelming at times in your life.*[10]

For the betterment of your husbands, the church, and the gospel, continue to hope in God and dedicate yourselves to submitting to your husbands out of obedience to God, honoring, assisting, encouraging, and supporting them. Confront them with grace, and counsel them with godly wisdom. In so doing, you demonstrate that you are truly daughters of Sarah who are precious in the sight of God.

Chapter 5

REPLANTING EDEN

1 Peter 3:7a

I'm not sure how long that tired old joke has traveled around—that marriage is a fine institution, if you're willing to be put in an institution.

Sadly, people are often in agreement with that derogatory view of marriage. In fact, according to recent polling, a large majority of people in the Western world view marriage as an outdated institution.[1] In our generation, we have reached the point where more couples are living together than marrying.

Frankly, our self-absorbed, self-promoting, self-serving world finds it difficult to surrender to the foundational principles of marriage—first and foremost of which is self-denial.

Yet marriage happens to be the most sanctifying relationship on the planet—or it can be—simply because it calls for men and women to die to self.

And that's especially, and explicitly, the case for men. The apostle Paul writes to husbands, "Love your wives like you love your own body; love your wives like you love yourself" (Ephesians 5:28 paraphrased).

He also gives the ultimate command when he tells husbands, "Love your wives, just as Christ also loved the church" (Ephesians 5:25). And if you're wondering what that might mean, Paul spells it out by adding, "and gave Himself up for her."

The ultimate act of self-denying love is Christ literally dying so that He can redeem sinners whom He calls His bride. That kind of sacrifice isn't partial. You don't partially die for someone; you don't die 60 percent and remain alive 40 percent. If you die, you're dead.

According to the Bible, marital love is tantamount to dying:

- dying to self-desire
- dying to self-ambition
- dying to self-preservation
- dying to self-promotion
- dying to self-will
- dying to a self-absorbing, self-satisfying lifestyle

A good marriage is a marriage that is constantly putting self to death. There's just no more room for yourself. This means, then, that a successful marriage isn't finding the right person; it's becoming the right person.

The Greek scholar R. C. H. Lenski made a thought-provoking statement about returning marriage to God's original design when he wrote nearly a hundred years ago, "Cure selfishness and you replant the Garden of Eden."[2]

This is why marriage, as defined by Scripture, is the greatest demonstration of the love of Christ—and the gospel—on the planet: it is selfless.

In 1 Peter 3, the apostle Peter describes this Christ-exalting marital relationship.

Peter began chapter 3 by calling on the wife to rank herself under her husband's leadership in voluntary submission. In our study we explained how this does not undermine her personal worth but actually expresses it. She has the unique opportunity to model Jesus Christ, who voluntarily submitted to the will of His Father in the plan of redemption. Jesus was, and is, co-eternal and co-equal in essence with God the Father. Jesus Christ is equally divine yet willingly submissive to the will of His Father.[3]

So a submissive wife, although equally valuable and co-equal to her husband in her standing in the gospel, models the heart and attitude of Christ in her submission.

The husband likewise has a unique opportunity to model Jesus Christ by giving his life in sacrificial love to win, keep, provide for, and care for his bride.

So, in a good marriage, both the husband and the wife are modeling different aspects of what we see in the life of our Lord.

Having spent six verses on wives, Peter now addresses husbands in a single verse. Yet as we will observe, this one verse for husbands is as loaded as the previous six verses for wives.

In fact, we can easily discern four different points in 1 Peter 3:7, and each one speaks volumes—convicting, transforming, and encouraging us.

First, there is a divine command: **You husbands in the same way, live with your wives in an understanding way.**

Second, there is a creation distinctive: **as with someone weaker, since she is a woman.**

Third is a prophetic incentive: **and show her honor as a fellow heir of the grace of life.**

Fourth, we find a spiritual ultimatum: **so that your prayers will not be hindered.**

We will look at just the first point in this chapter.

PROPER ATTITUDE

At the beginning of verse 7, we find the words **in the same way**, or "likewise" as some versions translate it. Peter is saying that just as there are things for the wife to do and act and live and obey, so, likewise, there are things for the husband to do and act and live and obey. In other words, a good marriage is never a one-way street.

And Peter begins his comments to husbands with a command: **Live with your wives in an understanding way.**

Before we dive into the meaning of understanding your wife, it is important that we understand this first expression: **Husbands . . . live with your wives.**

Peter isn't saying, "Live in the same neighborhood." This isn't a reference to an address; it's a reference to an attitude.[4]

This verbal form, which is found only here in the Greek New Testament, implies much more than living under the same roof. One author says the nearest equivalent in the English language is "making a home for."[5]

As we might put it, the expression makes the distinction between a house and a home. Peter is essentially saying, "Husbands, make your house a home with your wife." And that requires much more than just bringing home the bacon. It requires husbands to bring themselves home. Live—dwell, commune—with your wife, Peter says.

I read recently that according to one survey, the average husband and wife talk to each other thirty-seven minutes *per week.*[6] That's a housing arrangement, not a home. That's surviving marriage, not growing the garden of marriage.

It's possible for a marriage to go on for years like that— half an hour of conversation a week. But that is sort of like enduring an armed truce. One author describes it as a situation where competition replaces cooperation. Unresolved conflict has worn away the fabric of the marriage, and the husband and wife are staying together for good reasons but never the best reasons.[7]

Many couples stay together for the sake of the children. That is commendable, but it is far from the best reason to remain together.

According to one story, an eighty-nine-year-old man and his wife were seeking a divorce. The astonished judge asked them, "Why, after all these years, do you now want a divorce?" They answered, "We wanted to wait until the children were dead."[8]

Decades earlier the weeds of life took over in that marriage and choked off the flowers of companionship and enjoyment—the kinds of things that blossom on the stems of commitment and humility and sacrificial love.

A garden of flowers never happens by accident. I love driving back into the state of North Carolina after being away. I don't know who's in charge of planning it—and I'm sure our taxes pay for it—but it isn't long before my wife and I notice at major interstate intersections and at off- and on-ramps along the interstate, there are beautiful gardens of flowers. Sometimes they are acres of beautiful wildflowers, and sometimes they're arrangements of flowers in a variety of colors.

As we drive past these colorful displays, we would never dream that any of them happened by accident. It took time, and then more time, and expense, and sweat, and more sweat, to make them happen.

In marriage, the same is true—and husbands happen to be the chief gardeners. Husbands must take the lead and replant the Garden of Eden.

PROPER UNDERSTANDING

Now notice, Peter writes, **Husbands . . . live with your wives in an understanding way.** Your translation might read, "Live with your wives according to knowledge."

The word for **understanding** here refers to insight and a conscious sensitivity.[9] It combines the ideas of intelligence through observation and then consideration in action.[10]

This kind of understanding doesn't develop in a moment. It takes a lifetime of study. And that might seem like an impossible task. After all, men often tell each other, "You just can't understand women. They are so complicated you just can't figure them out."

It is interesting that wives are never told to understand their husbands. Maybe that's because women are naturally more intuitive and observant and don't need such a command. They pick up on everything, constantly watching and weighing data. Men just want to know what's for supper.

But here is an interesting point: The Bible does not require a man to understand *women*. God commands him to understand one woman—his wife! And that's a lifelong, self-denying, self-giving, gospel-demonstrating, Christ-modeling process.

And keep in mind, as one author pointed out, this command isn't simply talking about superficial understanding or knowledge—surface knowledge—like her favorite ice cream flavor or her favorite color. What Peter is talking about is knowing her challenges and desires and needs and then acting on that knowledge by assisting and encouraging and guiding her through life.[11]

This is where the husband operates in the home like a shepherd, shepherding her to her final home. He is attempting to carry the burdens of life rather than create them.

Earlier in this chapter, Peter did not tell wives to respect and follow their husbands and to have a gentle and quiet spirit *only if* their husbands are loving or are followers of

Christ. Indeed, women are commanded to do these things despite the fact that their husbands are unbelievers, undeserving of the deepest respect a godly husband would engender.

And now, husbands, the same shoe fits here as well. Peter is not suggesting that if your wife has a gracious spirit and respects and follows you, then you are to find ways to show intelligent and caring consideration to her. No, you are commanded to observe her needs and move to fulfill them even if she treats you with disrespect and an ungracious spirit.[12]

Marriage is not a quid-pro-quo arrangement—if you scratch my back, I'll scratch your back; if you're good to me, I'll be good to you; if you're loving and kind to me, I'll be loving and kind to you. Listen, it's easy to love the loving. It's easy to care for the caring. It's easy to be gracious to the gracious.

But a marriage limited to such if-then thinking never moves forward because no one will step on the gas and take the initiative.

Men, step on the gas!

"How?" you might ask. "I mean, I don't understand much about her at all!"

The command of Peter here implies that you act upon what you *do* understand. Then continue to live with her and talk with her and walk with her through life and gain more understanding, and then act upon that too.

That's self-denying love and is the first command in verse 7.

Remember what Lenski wrote: "Cure selfishness and you replant the Garden of Eden."

PRACTICAL SUGGESTIONS

As with previous chapters, let me suggest a couple of practical garden tools to use in your own private Garden of Eden.

Don't Be Thoughtless—Plant Seeds of Politeness

In other words, don't be rude, or unkind.

After a man attended a seminar on efficiency, he decided he would help his wife make her life more efficient too. A few days later he was telling a coworker who had also attended the seminar how it was going. He said, "One morning as I sat at the breakfast table watching my wife make breakfast, I realized I'd watched her do the same inefficient routine for years. She made lots of trips to the refrigerator, stove, table, and cabinets, often carrying just a single item at a time. So I said, 'Honey, why don't you eliminate all that legwork by carrying more than one item at a time?'" The guy's friend asked, "Did it save time?" He said, "Yes, it did; it used to take her twenty minutes to get breakfast ready; now I do it in seven."

Along this same line, the apostle Paul adds this note to husbands: "Husbands, love your wives and do not be embittered against them" (Colossians 3:19).

The word translated "embittered" carries the idea of being harsh or sharp-tongued.[13] One author writes that Paul's statement refers to a man who has arrived at an embittered state and all he can do is act out with impatience and thoughtlessness.[14]

This is a man who has become so filled with himself that he really doesn't care anymore if his wife is hurt or happy, crying or contented. In fact, he almost dares her to trouble him with her troubles!

A news article I came across some time ago was rather comical on one hand but sad on the other. A couple in Germany had been married for decades; he was seventy-two years old, and his wife was elderly as well. He had hooked up an air-raid siren in his house to stun his wife into silence. CNN reported that whenever this man's wife complained or tried to get on to him about something, he cranked up the siren and let it rip for a few minutes. After complaints from neighbors, the police arrived and told him to take down the siren. He complied reluctantly because, as he told the police, "It works every time."

You might not have an air-raid siren, but unkind, impolite, and inconsiderate actions will speak louder than words—and even sirens.

There's no excuse for a rude, discourteous, uncouth demeanor for a man in public—much less for a husband in private. Men, this will not only hurt your marriage but will also do harm to your ministry and the gospel you represent, the gospel of *grace*.

Hudson Taylor, the renowned missionary to China over a century ago, bemoaned this missing quality of politeness. He himself was known for his sensitivity toward Chinese culture. In fact, early on in his ministry, he created a sensation when he died his hair black, put on the que, or pigtail, and the gown and slippers of a traditional Chinese teacher. He would write later in life, "Rude Christians will seldom be out of hot water in China and although they are earnest and pious, they will not accomplish much. In nothing do we fail more, as a Mission, than in a lack of politeness."[15]

Husbands, plant seeds of politeness, and pull out the weeds of thoughtlessness.

Don't Be Abusive—Plant Seeds of Affirmation

Abuse comes in many forms—emotional, verbal, and physical. It comes from the mouths and hands of men who are angry with their own inadequacies and are attempting to boost their self-importance by bullying, pushing, and demanding people step aside and make room for them at the top.[16] And the wife is most often at the tip of this spear.

I have read that recent data indicate that one out of every six adult women have experienced or are currently experiencing some sort of verbal or physical abuse.

This kind of male domination has nothing to do with biblical headship. It has nothing to do with God's creation and everything to do with man's corruption.

Biblical headship isn't driving; it's leading. It isn't coercion; it's modeling humility and grace.

In commenting on this text, the authors of a recent book remind us that Jesus Christ, our perfect Groomsman, does not coerce the church, His bride. He woos the church and loves her by laying His life down for her. He wins her heart and brings her to glad obedience. He isn't harsh or manipulative but loving and gracious for the good of the church and the glory of His Father.[17]

If you want to live with your wife with kindness and consideration, begin building verbal bridges instead of verbal walls.[18]

One man suggested with humor, "Try praising your wife even if it does frighten her at first."[19]

Replace abusive words with affirming words. Just try one affirming word a day, for starters. Affirming someone else prunes back pride and plants seeds of humility.

How about saying, "Thank you"? Those words require humility because they remind you that you needed something that your wife provided.

When's the last time you thanked your wife for anything? So start tonight with supper—even if you frighten her. She'll wonder who's inhabiting your body. "Thank you, sweetheart, for supper; it was delicious." And if it wasn't delicious, you can say, "Thank you, sweetheart, for supper; it was . . . unforgettable."

Say affirming words to your wife like, "I'm so glad God gave you to me."

That's the opposite of what Adam meant in his Garden of Eden when he effectively complained, "Lord, look at this woman you gave me." Imagine what that did to Eve.

Say words I believe Adam said later on: "Will you forgive me?"

Will you forgive me? That's pride-killing language; imagine, an admission of wrong from the man of the house.

Those are ego-crushing, humility-planting words of grace and growth. Say them often!

I've heard it said—and it's probably true—that it takes eight to ten positive comments to offset just one destructive comment. In other words, eight to ten kind words are needed to erase the effects of just one hurtful, unkind, unloving, careless word that was written on the tablet of someone's memory.

Invest in the garden of your own wife and family and home. In fact, make up your mind when you come home to bring yourself with you. You've had a long day. You've faced untold challenges. Follow the advice of Dennis Rainey's friend, who has a simple three-by-five card on his desk that reads, "Leave some for home."[20] In other words, save some energy and investment for home.

You've got a garden to grow at home. Your wife waits for the chief gardener to arrive and roll up his sleeves and plant some new seeds along the way.

There's a song that describes the commitment of a husband who follows the counsel of 1 Peter 3 and continues to learn to deny himself and lay down his life for his wife. It goes like this:

> *Tomorrow morning if you wake up*
> *And the sun does not appear*
> *I, I will be here*
>
> *If in the dark, we lose sight of love*
> *Hold my hand, and have no fear*
> *'Cause I, I will be here*

I will be here
When you feel like being quiet
When you need to speak your mind
I will listen

And I will be here
When the laughter turns to cryin'
Through the winning, losing and trying
We'll be together
I will be here

Tomorrow morning, if you wake up
And the future is unclear
I will be here

Just as sure as seasons were made for change
Our lifetimes were made for these years
So I will be here
I will be here

And you can cry on my shoulder
When the mirror tells us we're older
I will hold you
And I will be here

To watch you grow in beauty
And tell you all the things you are to me
I will be here

I will be true to the promise I have made
To you and to the One who gave you to me

Tomorrow morning, if you wake up
And the sun does not appear
I will be here.[21]

In the context of 1 Peter, this is the kind of lifestyle that makes the world take note and say, "There is something different about Christianity. There is something different about that couple's marriage. There is something very different about the way that man treats his wife. Man, I need to find out what it is."

And we get to tell them *who* it is that makes the difference, *who* it is who loves us with unfailing love: our Lord Jesus Christ, the One who will always be here.

Chapter 6

THE ORIGINAL MANUAL ON MANHOOD

1 Peter 3:7b

I don't think we could ever find a more politically incorrect passage of Scripture on the subject of manhood and womanhood—much less on marriage—than the inspired words of the apostle Peter in the third chapter of his first epistle. Our interest, however, is in what is biblically correct, not what is politically correct, so I direct your attention back to God's original manual on manhood in 1 Peter 3:7.

I would like to quote at length from the opening chapter of John Piper's little booklet entitled, *What's the Difference? Manhood and Womanhood Defined According to the Bible.*

> When I was a boy growing up in Greenville, South Carolina, my father was away from home about two-thirds of every year. And while he preached across the country, we prayed—my mother, and my older sister and I. What I learned in those days was that my mother was omni-competent.
>
> She handled the finances, paying all the bills and dealing with the bank and the creditors. She once ran a little laundry business on the side. She was

active on the park board, and served as the superintendent of the intermediate department of our Southern Baptist church . . .

She taught me how to cut the grass and splice electric cord and pull Bermuda grass by the roots and paint the eaves and shine the dining-room table with a shammy and drive a car and keep French fries from getting soggy in the cooking oil. She helped me with the maps in geography and showed me how to do a bibliography and believe that Algebra II was possible. . . .

I heard one time that women don't sweat, they glow. . . . My mother sweated. It would drip off the end of her long, sharp nose. Sometimes she would blow it off when her hands were pushing the wheelbarrow full of peat moss. Or she would wipe it with her sleeve between the strokes of a swingblade. . . .

But it never occurred to me [as a boy] to think of my mother and father in the same category. Both were strong. Both were bright. Both were kind. Both would kiss me and both would spank me. . . . Both prayed with fervor and loved the Bible.

But unmistakably my father was a man and my mother was a woman. They knew it and I knew it. And it was not mainly a biological fact. It was mainly a matter of personhood and relational dynamics.

When my father came home he was clearly the head of the house. He led in prayer at the table. He called the family together for devotions. He got us to Sunday school and worship. He drove the car. He guided the family to where we would sit. He made the decision to go to Howard Johnson's for lunch. He led us to the table. He called for the waitress. He paid the check. He was the one we knew we would reckon with if we broke a family rule or were disrespectful to Mother.

These were the happiest times for Mother. Oh, how she rejoiced to have Daddy home. She loved his leadership. Later I learned that the Bible calls this "submission." . . .

It never occurred to me that leadership and submission had anything to do with superiority [or] inferiority. . . . It was not a matter of capabilities and competencies. . . .

Over the years I have come to see from Scripture and from life that manhood and womanhood are the beautiful handiwork of a good and loving God. He [actually] designed our differences, and they are profound . . . They go to the root of [who we are].[1]

Well said.

The climactic creative act of our Creator God was not the creation of the elephants, giraffes, dolphins, or birds or the trees, rivers, and lakes. The climactic moment of creation occurred when God designed and crafted and created them male and female (Genesis 1:27)

That was the grand finale of the Genesis creation account. Maleness and femaleness, with all their nuances, complexities, abilities, and inabilities, were a part of the glorious creation of God. And the manual God has given us through inspiration describes us as male or female persons, not because of culture or convention, but because of divine creation.

CULTURAL CONFUSION

I want to make a simple statement but one that might seem rather earthshaking in light of the current confusion in our culture.

Here it is: *In His creative design, God never intended to separate anatomy from identity.[2]*

Anatomy and identity are bound together in personhood—what makes you, you and me, me.

Yes, because of sin, there is within human nature the capacity for all kinds of aberrations and inclinations and dispositions and desires and mannerisms and the potential for every evil and defiant act against God imaginable. But being fundamentally male or female is a gift from God, who knit you together in the womb according to His purposes.

In addition to sinful human nature, which tends to pervert God's creative purposes, Satan is at work, spreading the propaganda of defiance. He hates the human race because humans are uniquely the image bearers of God. Satan wants to destroy that which represents the pinnacle of God's creation. That means divorce isn't his end game; homosexuality and lesbianism aren't his end game; same-sex marriage isn't his end game; surrogate motherhood isn't his end game; bisexuality isn't his end game; transgenderism and gender fluidity aren't his end game.

Satan wants to destroy the peak of God's glorious creation by striking at the heart of the divine design for humans—*Satan wants to eliminate the concept of gender altogether.*

We are now observing his all-out attack on male and female distinctions, an attack that has been quite successful. Indeed, today it is terribly out of date to speak of manhood and womanhood in any kind of fixed sense. Gender is now considered fluid; fluidity has replaced biology. There is no specific foundation or meaning for manhood or womanhood, and that means there is no longer any structure or plan.[3]

Gender confusion is now a growing epidemic. And the consequences are already becoming catastrophic. There are more sexual perversions and aberrations claiming normality today, not less; there is more abuse and promiscuity, not less; there is more social awkwardness and distress, not less; there is more despair and there are more suicides today, not less.[4]

Still, our culture continues to defy the Creator. School systems in the Western world are racing to avoid any kind of gender-specific language. In one program, under the title, "Welcoming Schools" the curriculum encourages teachers to "use their 'unique and influential role' to create conditions where children feel safe in . . . 'expressing and identifying their gender.'"[5]

The key word is *identifying*. Children need to decide whether they're little boys or little girls. It's little wonder that transgender-affirming children's books are at the heart of this program, which openly coaches teachers to "teach and affirm gender fluidity."[6]

One school counselor said that her school's inclusive policies have eliminated gender-specific language and activities. She cites one illustration: there are no more "'Muffins for Mom' and 'Donuts for Dad'—it's just 'Muffin Mornings' and 'Donut Day.'"[7]

A few years ago, a school system in England renamed the gingerbread man the gingerbread people on school lunch menus in four hundred schools. Only in response to a public outcry was the gingerbread man given back his name.

Here's the bigger issue—much bigger than the gingerbread man—the male and female sexes have lost the script for their lives and no longer know what roles to play in life.

We need to go back and pick up the script . . . written and produced by the Creator. And we will find that the original manual teaches just the opposite of today's culture, which is racing to eliminate gender distinctions.

BIBLICAL CLARITY

Listen to these gender-affirming words coming directly from God's original manual on manhood and womanhood.

You husbands in the same way, live with your wives in an understanding way, as with someone weaker, since she is a woman. (1 Peter 3:7)

Notice that phrase: **as with someone weaker, since she is a woman.** In one politically incorrect phrase, Peter defies contemporary culture and defends God's created order.

Several observations from this text jump out at us:

- Peter is violating the shrine of gender neutrality by making a statement of gender distinction.
- Peter is clearly saying that women are weaker than men.
- Peter is clearly telling men that they are supposed to treat women differently than men.
- Peter clearly states that the female sex is genetically and anatomically and inherently different from the male.

Peter would never be invited to speak to the local PTA.

Now at first glance it might sound like Peter is condemning or demeaning women. Certainly to ears trained by society's propaganda, it sounds like he is. But he isn't. He's doing nothing more than telling men to act like men and women to expect to be treated like women. And, specifically, he's saying a man should treat a woman differently than he would treat another man.

In fact, Peter is indirectly challenging all men, not just husbands. This is evident because textually Peter is addressing the issue of women in general and how they should be treated. It's also clear that a man doesn't become a man when he gets married. Therefore, this is not just a manual on marriage but a manual on manhood.

And God's manual on manhood has a lot to do with how men treat women.

As we saw in the previous chapter, Peter opens this verse by commanding the husband to live with his wife with understanding; that is, with insight, with consideration. Peter now explains why this is necessary.

Treat Your Wife as Weaker

First, Peter declares that the woman is **weaker.**

But what does it mean that a woman is **someone weaker** ("weaker vessel" is a better translation) than a man?

Well, it's really not that hard to figure out. As someone once said, "It's not rocket surgery."

The word for **weaker** (*asthenēs*) simply indicates that, in general, the average woman is physically weaker than the average man.[8] Peter is speaking in general terms about the female sex in contrast to the male.

And if you don't like that interpretation, you're left with wondering whether Peter is telling us here that women are intellectually weaker, morally weaker, mentally weaker, spiritually weaker, theologically weaker, or weaker in their resolve or in their faith. Such interpretations might suggest, as some have claimed, that the Bible teaches that women are inferior to men.

That's not what Peter says. Physical weakness is not the same thing as inferiority.

In fact, Peter makes it very clear later in this verse that a woman is as much a child of God and as equally deserving of being rewarded in the coming kingdom as are believing men. She is a "fellow heir of the grace of life."

Peter is delivering a general statement about the physical makeup of the average woman contrasted to the physical makeup of the average man. In general, she can't throw as hard, run as fast, or lift as much.

But what's interesting is that the word Peter uses here in the Greek text for a weaker vessel (*skeuos*) is used by Paul in referring to household vessels, or utensils (2 Timothy 2:20).[9] Paul also uses the word to refer to the physical body (1 Thessalonians 4:4).

So Peter is simply stating in general terms to husbands especially, and to men in general, they should be careful and kind and considerate in the way they treat their wives, in particular, and all women in general.

In other words, don't blur the basic distinctions between men and women, which God intended to highlight. Instead, acknowledge and enjoy them. The original manual from God doesn't remove the concepts of masculinity and femininity but commands us to respect them.

Referring to women as the weaker sex, as coined by Peter here, isn't derogatory or demeaning. Peter isn't diminishing the value of women; in fact, he is essentially commanding men to treat women with distinction and consideration and kindness. In blunt terms, he's saying. "Men, don't treat women like a bunch of guys because they aren't a bunch of guys."

Men are not to exploit them but to honor them, treating them with courtesy and deference.[10]

Treat Your Wife as a Woman

Why are women to be treated this way? Well, for starters, because they happen to be women—**since she is a woman**, Peter writes. In other words, women deserve that kind of courtesy and kindness and deference because of the simple fact that they are women.

As strange as it sounds, Peter is commanding the husband to treat his wife like a woman.

Let's get as practical as we can here: What exactly does it look like to treat a wife like a woman?

Obviously, Peter has described it for us as consideration and understanding, which means kindness and courtesy. But let's answer that question by giving the opposite of what it looks like.

1.   *Treating your wife like a woman is the opposite of apathy.*

You can call apathy indifference, unconcern for her needs and well-being, irritation rather than interest, criticism instead of commendation. Call it failure to step up to the plate, failure to provide and protect.

There's an old Hebrew proverb from the Talmud that gives this great advice: Every husband should eat and drink beneath his means, clothe himself within his means, and honor his wife above his means.

Treating your wife like a woman is the opposite of apathy.

2. *Treating your wife like a woman is the opposite of absence.*

You can call this absence self-centeredness, where her activities never matter and yours are never missed. This isn't just failing to step up to the plate; it's living as if there's no plate at all . . . or no ball game at all.

Absence is when your involvement in your hobbies and sports activities are measured in hours, but your involvement with your wife and family is measured in minutes.

I love the unusual sentence a Florida judge handed down to a husband in a recent case involving a domestic dispute with his wife. Evidently an argument had broken out on her birthday. Well, the judge ended up telling the husband that he needed to figure out a plan for marriage counseling, but in the meantime, the judge said, "On your way home from this courthouse, you are to pick up some flowers for your wife, along with a birthday card; go home and deliver them to your wife; then both of you are to get dressed up and you are to take your wife out to dinner at Red Lobster (not Taco Bell this time, but Red Lobster), and after taking her out to Red Lobster for dinner, take her bowling."

His attorney jokingly asked, "Does he have to let her win?"

The judge didn't smile back but said that if his client failed to comply, he'd be back in court.

3. *Treating your wife like a woman is the opposite of abuse.*

Abuse can take the form of verbal intimidation or physical threats or outright physical abuse. It is using your strength to your advantage to bully and dominate your wife in order to get your way.

Evidently, what began in the playground sandbox with other kids when you didn't get your way was something you never outgrew.

Listen to the words of Paul to the believing men in the Corinthian congregation: "Act like men; be strong" (1 Corinthians 16:13).

Act like men. What a concept! Act like men, not like boys and not like women. Like Peter, Paul recognizes that there is a specific way a man should act; namely, with manly bravery. "Stand firm in the faith," he writes. He's not asking men to be macho; he's asking men to be mature.[11]

Like Peter, Paul is challenging every male in the early church—and to this day—to effectively grow up and act like men.

Acting like a man is not throwing your weight around. It's not yielding to selfish anger by yelling and slamming and throwing and name calling and cursing or even huffing and snorting when you don't get your way or your wife gets in your way.[12]

Acting like a man, in relation to your wife is using your strength to make sure she is treated with respect and deference.

One Greek scholar pointed out that Peter's use of the word for **woman** in this text is unusual; it is an adjective that serves as an abstract. In other words, it refers to the female nature; thus, Peter is referring to the fact that she is womanly,[13] or as we might say, "since she is feminine."

Now that doesn't mean she isn't as tough as nails. When Peter calls her a weaker vessel, keep in mind that he does not call her weak.

Have you ever been in a delivery room? I can tell you who the weaker one is at that moment—at least in my case, it wasn't my wife.

I came across a wonderful example of a mother's courage, evidenced in her determination to save her little boy from harm. A couple built a home on the banks of a small pond at the headwaters of a creek in Florida, not far from the Gulf of Mexico. Their twelve-year-old son, Michael, loved to snorkel in the two-acre pond, and one evening, he and two of his cousins went for a swim just after dinner. Oblivious to any danger, they were unaware that an alligator was bearing down on them.

This couple and some neighbors who were out in the backyard spotted the alligator and tried to distract it with clapping and shouting. This alerted the cousins, and they made it to shore. But Michael was snorkeling, and his head was under the water as he floated peacefully along. The alligator lunged for Michael's head. It missed, but gashed Michael's skull, ripping the snorkel mask from his face. He began swimming for shore as fast as he could.

Only momentarily diverted by the mask, the alligator spotted the boy and was after him again. By this time Michael's mother had run to the water's edge, where her son was in a race for his life. He was swimming as fast as he could, but the alligator was gaining on him every second. The mother reached out to grasp her son's hand just as the beast opened its huge jaws and clamped down on Michael's left leg.

What followed was a tug of war between an eleven-foot alligator and a five-and-a-half-foot mother. Clutching her boy's hand, she pulled with every ounce of strength she had, and suddenly, unexpectedly, the alligator let go. Perhaps the rubber flipper on her son's foot had agitated the alligator's throat, but for whatever reason, Michael was saved.

Six months later, his wounds completely healed, Michael was showing his scars to his friends—the scar on his scalp and the scars still visible on the ankle of his left leg, which had been broken but was now mended. But the scars he was most proud of, which he showed his friends, were the scars in his hand that had been made by his mother's fingernails. She had literally dug into his flesh to keep him from being dragged away.[14]

That was one determined woman.

Listen, being weaker doesn't mean being weak. It has nothing to do with resolve and determination; it has to do with her nature and general disposition.

In fact, Peter's use of the phrase here, literally, "a **weaker** vessel," can be understood in the sense of refinement. In other words, she is weaker in the sense that she has been created as more refined.

One author takes this idea and paraphrases it this way: "Treat your wife like fine china."[15]

There's a difference between a cheap mug and fine china. The truth is, you drink coffee from a cheap mug differently than you do from a fine china teacup. That is why men go for the cheap mug every time. Fine china is simply handled differently.

One author wrote that you can understand this analogy to mean that you are to treat your wife like you would treat an expensive vase (vaze).

You spend a little money at Wal-Mart for a vase; you spend a lot of money on it, and it's a "vaze." Treat her like an expensive "vaze."

Don't miss this here: Peter is essentially challenging husbands to stop abusive actions and speech. They are never to pummel their wives with their hands or their words. She's effectively an expensive "vase" and is to be treated that way.

Abusive speech, physical intimidation and threats, and even physical harm—these aren't things to gloss over or quickly dismiss.

If you're like a bull in a china shop and pieces are littered on the floor of your home life, reach out to another brother for help and accountability.

Don't excuse yourself. Don't blame your bad day at work or even your wife's behavior. That's Adam in the garden, his mouth dripping with forbidden fruit, telling God, "It was that woman You gave me . . . she made me."

That's how boys act. Men take responsibility for their actions. Start acting like a man.[16]

Let me add this for women of all ages: If you are being physically or verbally or sexually abused, what you are experiencing is not your fault. It's not acceptable, and it's not a secret you have to keep. It's not only a sinful act against you; it's dangerous and destructive, and it will only escalate and crush and destroy. Let the church—the leaders in the church and your brothers and sisters in the church—provide help and counsel and assistance for you and others who are caught in the painful web of an abusive relationship.

CALL TO LOVE

There should be no question what it means to occupy the role of a man. God's original manual on manhood makes it clear how men are to treat women in general and especially and uniquely their wives—because they are women.

This is really a call to love them as Christ loves His bride, the church—with strong, committed, caring, persevering, humble, faithful love.

That mirrors the Creator's love for us, doesn't it? That's all that Peter is really saying to husbands here: start loving your wives like God loves us all.

One day Charles Spurgeon, the famous pastor in nineteenth-century London, was walking through the English countryside with a friend. As they strolled along, Spurgeon noticed a barn with a weather vane on its roof. As they got closer, they noticed etched into the weather vane were the words, "God is love." Spurgeon remarked to his friend that he thought this was an inappropriate place for such a message. He said, "Weather vanes are changeable— always turning with the wind." His friend responded, "No Charles, I think you misunderstand the meaning. That weather vane is indicating a truth: regardless of which way the wind blows, God is love."[17]

"Husbands," Paul wrote to the Ephesians, "love your wives, just as Christ also loved the church" (5:25) . . . no matter how the wind blows.

Live with them with kind consideration, for they are weaker vessels. They've been created and are to be treated like fine china. That's how a real man treats a woman, and more specifically, that's how a husband treats his wife.

And brothers, there has never been a better time for men of God to be just that—*men* of God.

Chapter 7

HOW TO TREAT ROYALTY

1 Peter 3:7c

Portuguese aristocrat Luis Carlos de Noronha Cabral da Camara (with a name like that you know he has to be rich) made an unusual last will and testament. Luis had never married and had no extended family. Thirteen years before his death, he met with his attorney and two witnesses to name the heirs of his estate.

He reached for the Lisbon phone book and began turning the pages, pointing to names at random without rhyme or reason—seventy names in all—and made them his heirs.

When he died, those seventy people were contacted. Many of them thought it was a scam and had to be convinced it was true—they were co-heirs with sixty-nine other people to the estate of Luis Carlos de Noronha Cabral da Camara.[1]

Can you imagine receiving a phone call informing you that you've been chosen by some millionaire as an heir of his vast estate?

One of the greatest oversights in the Christian life is that every believer has a future inheritance that boggles the imagination. Every Christian has inherited the vast estate of heaven and all the riches of God, through our Relative by faith—Jesus Christ. Yet we so often take it for granted. We go through our day hardly thinking of the fact that we're going to live as royalty, ruling and reigning in the coming, global kingdom of God.

In God's plan, this truth is a significant incentive for us to act the part of a royal heir, here and now. Indeed, nearly all the New Testament writers, inspired by the Spirit of God, allude to this great truth.

James writes, "Listen, my beloved brethren: did not God choose the poor of this world to be . . . heirs of the kingdom?" (James 2:5).

Paul wrote to the Roman believers, "We are children of God, and if children, heirs also, heirs of God and fellow heirs with Christ" (Romans 8:16-17).

You see, in legal terms, Jesus is not just our advocate; He is our brother. He's our elder brother, in biblical terminology. He's related to us, since by faith we are members of the family of God. In Hebrews 2:11, we are told that Jesus is not ashamed to call us His brethren—that is, His brothers and sisters.

That is the legal foundation for the apostles' declaration that we are fellow heirs of Jesus Christ.

So, consider this your phone call—ahead of time. You are being informed that you are a co-inheritor, a fellow heir, with Jesus Christ. You will share in the inheritance of Christ in eternity, along with all the other royal heirs who belong to the family of God. And this isn't by random chance!

So mark it down mentally: you are royalty; you just haven't inherited the full measure of it yet.

But it won't be long, beloved, before you and I are looking at each other and laughing and rejoicing and singing and praising God over who we've become, what we've been given, where we're going to live, and how we're going to spend eternity as heirs to the riches and the splendor and the grace of God.

This is no small-scale incentive for today. It is a truth God wants to use to transform our thinking and shape our perspective and encourage us as we suffer and persevere through the challenges and struggles of life.

Don't lose sight of your unbelievable, incredible inheritance.

In fact, that's how the apostle Peter began his first letter—telling us about our imperishable, unfading inheritance that is being kept for us in heaven (1 Peter 1:4).

Now, in chapter 3 the apostle again brings up this truth that we are heirs. But this time he uses it to challenge the thinking and behavior of every married man in the body of Christ.

We have been looking at 1 Peter 3:7:

You husbands in the same way, live with your wives in an understanding way, as with someone weaker, since she is a woman; and show her honor as a fellow heir of the grace of life, so that your prayers will not be hindered.

In this verse we have observed the command to husbands, **Live with your wives**, which means to make a home with them. Men are homemakers too in a literal sense, making a home with their wives. They are to do this **in an**

understanding way; that is, with kindness and consideration, recognizing that the wife is **weaker, since she is a woman**. Peter doesn't say that she is *weak* but that she is *weaker*. We studied the practical implications of the creation of gender in our last chapter. Now notice the final words of verse 7:

> . . . **and show her honor as a fellow heir of the grace of life, so that your prayers will not be hindered.**

Peter concludes his instructions to wives and husbands by delivering to every husband a daily assignment, a prophetic announcement, and a serious advisement.

DAILY ASSIGNMENT

Notice, first, the daily assignment: **Show her honor.**

The present tense of the verb tells us this is to be an ongoing practice, not something done just on her birthday or anniversary. This is a daily activity.

We can understand this to mean *assign her honor.*[2] This is the only time this compound participle appears in the New Testament, but it has the idea of assigning to someone something the person is due.[3]

The expression clearly implies an assessment of the wife's high value. And this high assessment isn't given because it's the nice-guy thing to do; it is directly related to who she is.

Not long ago, Marsha and I moved into an apartment for four months while we put our home through some major first-floor renovations. At the heart of the renovation was adding an elevator and building a library space large enough to house my library of some 6,000 volumes. For the first time in twenty years, my entire library was available to me in one location.

Because of the added square footage, we had an appraiser come to do an assessment as we prepared for refinancing. The appraiser was a young lady with a tablet and a tape measure in hand. She was thorough and careful. She wanted to know everything we had added to the house, every upgrade and change.

And I was glad she was interested. Obviously, the higher the appraisal, the greater the equity value in our home.

So I told her everything that was good about our nineteen-year-old house. I spread out the architectural plans on the counter and pointed out the width of this and the square footage of that. I was pointing out everything—even the new ceiling fan and the LED replacement light fixtures in the living room.

I didn't think I was bothering her or in her way, but my first clue was when she told me it would be okay if I went back to work.

I was convinced our home was not going to get the appraisal I knew it deserved. I was afraid she had overlooked something or didn't take something into account.

Now here's the question for you husbands: Is your wife getting an appraisal that God knows she deserves?

What might you be overlooking? What are you missing? Do you understand her true value?

Through the apostle Peter, God is telling husbands to assign their wives honor . . . to give their wives the highest appraisal in the neighborhood.

A husband is to show his wife honor to the highest degree![4]

And note this: Peter isn't telling husbands to *decide* if their wives have earned or deserve this high appraisal; he's telling husbands to *give* them that kind of appraisal daily and to act accordingly, simply because she is a believing wife.

Let me change the analogy for a moment. This word for **honor** was also used in New Testament days to describe a great treasure or a valuable gemstone.[5]

So how do you fulfill this daily assignment of handling your wife like a valuable treasure? There are at least two ways this should be lived out in your life.

First, you honor her by the way you talk about her. How do you talk about your wife at work . . . on the golf course . . . in front of the kids . . . to your extended family? In fact, how do you talk about her to her?

Second, you honor her by the way you provide for her. One Greek scholar pointed out that this word for **honor**, in noun form, gives us the word *honorarium*—compensation.[6]

It has a financial undertone to it, so depending on the context, it can relate to money.

Husbands, be generous.

One of the men in our church family sent me this story. Doug Smith was on his deathbed and knew the end was near. His hospice nurse, his wife, his daughter, and two sons were with him in the bedroom, waiting for his last breath.

He roused himself and asked for the nurse to write down his last wishes. He began: "To my son, Bernie, I want you to take the Mayfair houses. To my daughter Sybil, you take the apartments over in the east end. To my son Jamie, you take all the offices over in City Centre. And to Sarah, my dear wife, please take all the residential buildings on the bank of the river." And with that he breathed his last.

The nurse was blown away by the generosity of these final wishes and said to the man's wife, "Mrs. Smith, your husband was an amazing, generous, thoughtful man to have worked so hard and then given you and your children all these properties."

The wife replied, "Not really. He just had a big paper route."

Instead of simply referring to property or money, the word Peter uses relates to protecting and guarding and providing for the wife like you would protect, guard, and provide for something you treasure.

You keep expensive jewelry in fabric-covered containers or drawers; you keep passports and deeds in safe places; you put special photographs in frames; you keep your rifles and your tennis racket and your golf clubs in safe places. You don't leave any of those things lying around. You don't treat treasure carelessly.

So, men, how are you protecting and guarding and taking care of your relationship with your wife? What value have you assigned her?

And why does God believe she deserves such honorable treatment? Why does God believe your wife is inherently worthy of the highest appraisal?

Well Peter, a married man himself, effectively says, "I thought you'd ask that question, so let me tell you why."

PROPHETIC ANNOUNCEMENT

Notice further in 1 Peter 3:7: **Show her honor as a fellow heir of the grace of life.**

In other words, this high appraisal given the wife isn't based on something she's earned. It's based on who she is.

She is a fellow heir. She stands to inherit equally the full measure of the gift of life. Many evangelical scholars take this inheritance context and connect it to 1 Peter 1:4 and suggest Peter is wanting every husband to look down the road to that moment when his bride will become crowned, bejeweled, and robed and seated as a bride of Christ.

She is a fellow heir, a joint-heir, of eternal life. Christian husbands, you're not just married to a woman; you are married to a royal heir who will live forever.

Peter is reminding every believing husband of every believing wife that he is actually chaperoning her on her way to that moment when he will hand her off to her Bridegroom and Lord.

How are you taking care of a future member of the bridal party of heaven?

As we have seen, while the husband has been given greater authority and accountability to God as the head of the home, when it comes to the gospel, spiritual privileges, and eternal importance and a crown and a throne in the coming kingdom, husbands and wives are co-regents, co-heirs, with Christ.[7]

When these words of Peter's were read in the first-century assembly, I have little doubt they caused quite a stir in the worship service. I can imagine women leaning toward each other, whispering . . . surprised . . . excited . . . mystified at this prophetic announcement. The gospel had already elevated women to an entirely new level they'd never seen before, but this was a staggering prophetic revelation of their future.

By the way, anyone who tells you Christianity has held women down doesn't know history.

In ancient Greek and Roman cultures, wives led quiet lives of misery. They had no personal rights, they were without legal protection, and they were exploited and treated like beasts of burden.

They were viewed by their Greek and Roman husbands as far beneath them in status and worth. The Athenian orator Demosthenes once said that mistresses were for pleasure and wives for raising legitimate heirs to the family name.

Even in Jewish culture during the days of the apostles, Jewish women were treated terribly. They had no legal rights, and men could divorce their wives for just about anything they might find displeasing. In fact, Jewish men would offer a typical morning prayer that included the phrase, "Blessed art Thou, O Lord, who has not made me a Gentile or a woman."[8]

The Greek and Roman view of women continues even today in cultures without a Christian influence. In Islamic countries, for example, women can be denied equal value and personal rights, the husband has the legal and religious right to beat his wife for disobedience, inheritance rights are half—at best—to that of male heirs, and on and on it goes.

It is the gospel that makes seismic changes in the value of a woman. One historian wrote, "The birth of Jesus was the turning point in the history of the woman."[9]

The gospel commands a husband to love his wife like he loves himself and—better yet—like his Lord loves the church (Ephesians 5:25, 28).

The gospel informs women that their inheritance in the coming kingdom isn't less than that of men. They are equally co-heirs in that coming glorious kingdom (1 Peter 3:7).

What is the value of a woman? Peter is delivering a prophetic announcement that declares her invaluable: Treat your wife like royalty . . . like a discovered treasure.

A man who had inherited a blanket from his aunt had never thought much of it. In fact, the blanket was usually thrown over a chair in the bedroom rather casually, where it had stayed for years . . . until the *Antiques Roadshow* came through Tucson.

His aunt had once told him it had belonged to Kit Carson, but he thought she was a little looney by then and had no idea. However, on a whim, he and his wife took the blanket to see if it was worth anything.

The appraiser that day almost fainted when he saw the blanket. Although he couldn't prove it once belonged to Kit Carson, it did indeed date back to the early 1800s. It was an original Navajo creation, only fifty of which remained in existence. The blanket was valued at $350,000 to $500,000. The couple later sold it at auction for much more than that.[10]

I have read that some people arrive at the *Antiques Roadshow* alone and leave surrounded by armed guards. What they had casually walked in with was now something to guard at all costs.

Men, make this kind of attitude your daily assignment. Listen carefully to this prophetic announcement and treasure your wives.

SERIOUS ADVISEMENT

Finally, Peter now delivers a very serious warning: **Show her honor as a fellow heir of the grace of life, so that your prayers will not be hindered.**

Wow!

This expression, **your prayers**, certainly can be understood broadly as the prayers of the household or the prayers of the couple. But in this text, **your prayers** has direct reference to the prayer life of the husbands themselves. Peter is assuming that every believing husband is going to want to be praying.[11] Yet if they do not show their wives proper honor, their prayers will be **hindered**.

But wait! There was no stern warning given to women who refuse to submit to and respect their husbands; there was no warning to them for failing in their responsibilities. So why this warning to husbands?

When you follow the teaching on the marital relationship through the New Testament, you understand that the wife represents the mystery of the church united with Christ, but the husband represents the mystery of Christ united with the church. This means that, at her best, the wife represents the church; but at his best, the husband represents Christ.

Let that sink in. The husband represents God incarnate in the home.

The stakes, then, are much higher for the husband.

- His faithfulness is much more foundational.
- His influence is much more critical.
- His failure is much more devastating.

Frankly, husbands, if you don't care about your wife, God doesn't care about your praying. **Your prayers will . . . be hindered.**

The word Peter uses for **hindered** is a Greek term used of making a road impassable.[12] Soldiers would blockade roads with boulders to impede the enemy.

Paul used the same word to explain that he'd been hindered from visiting the Roman church earlier (Romans 15:22). He told the Thessalonians he'd been hindered more than once in his efforts to return to them (1 Thessalonians 2:18). Paul further used the word to rebuke the Christians in Galatia, asking them who had hindered them from advancing (Galatians 5:7). In other words, what got in the way of your spiritual progress?

The word also carries the idea of cutting in or interrupting.[13] There could hardly be a more serious divine threat than this: that all the promises of prayers heard and answered could be interrupted.[14]

Prayers are hindered, the Holy Spirit is grieved, and the enemy of the gospel is given opportunity to blockade the paths of spiritual progress and effectual prayer—these are devastating consequences for a man's failure to properly honor his wife.[15]

Consider the implications:

- The man who sins against his wife in knowingly refusing to show her consideration and honor and kindness finds a barrier between him and God.
- In other words, don't go to God as if everything's all right if you don't care enough to go to your wife to make things right.
- If you're not interested in listening to the needs of your wife, God isn't interested in listening to the needs in your life.
- Your marriage is actually an excellent barometer of the reality of your Christianity.

People at church or at work might say you are a wonderful Christian man. But that doesn't matter nearly as much as what your wife says about you in the home.

What's your wife's assessment of the reality of your Christianity? I can guarantee it has a lot to do with your assessment of the value of your wife.

You see, according to Peter, your fellowship with God is related to your fellowship with your wife. If you are out of fellowship with God, it means you'll be out of fellowship with your wife.

We men know that all too well. When we get out of fellowship with God, it doesn't take long before everybody in the household knows about it.

But here's Peter's point: When you act sinfully and proudly and selfishly and you don't care about living with your wife with courtesy and kindness—when you are out of fellowship with your wife—you are, in fact, out of fellowship with God.

Guaranteed.

Brothers, when you offend your wife, you offend God.[16]

This is a bigger deal than we might have thought.

Are we partners with our wives or competitors? Is your wife your servant, placed on the planet to meet your every need, or do you view her as a fellow heir of the coming kingdom—someone God has allowed you to chaperone with kindness to heaven?

Let's be honest. Because of our fallen nature, these seven verses in 1 Peter 3 are an uphill climb. Wives will struggle with respecting and following the lead of their husbands;

husbands will prefer their agendas and egos over the needs and feelings of their wives.[17] Marriage can become competition rather than cooperation.

One author wrote, "Domestic harmony doesn't come easy. Sometimes it feels downright impossible."[18]

Indeed.

Just don't give up. Rely daily on the power of the Spirit, and die daily to the pride of self. Stay at it even through hurtful times and disappointing times—and there will be many.

Learn to confess quickly when you fail. Readjust your appraisal because it tends to slip. Press on; don't quit.

Ladies, you are married to a royal son, and men, you are married to a regal daughter of the King.

And just think—one day you will witness the coronation of your spouse, a co-regent with Christ. And you will join your beloved as all the redeemed take their places in the bridal party at the marriage supper of the Lamb.

We will all shout with joy—unrestrained, unbridled joy—as we inherit the glory of God's presence and the wonder of God's kingdom and beyond that . . . eternal life!

In the meantime, stay the course and keep your vows!

ENDNOTES

Chapter 1

1 Paul David Tripp, *What Did You Expect?* (Crossway, 2010), 16.

2 Daniel M. Doriani, *1 Peter* (P&R, 2014), 108.

3 Evan Real, "Scarlett Johansson Says It's Not 'Natural' to Be Monogamous," *US Weekly*, February 14, 2017.

4 Charles R. Swindoll, *Insights on James and 1 & 2 Peter* (Zondervan, 2010), 185.

5 D. Edmond Hiebert, *1 Peter* (BMH, 1984), 195.

6 Ibid., 194.

7 Warren W. Wiersbe, *Be Hopeful: 1 Peter* (David C. Cook, 1982), 81.

8 John Piper, "Husbands Who Love Like Christ and the Wives Who Submit to Them" (sermon preached at Bethlehem Baptist Church, 6-11-1989).

9 John MacArthur, *1 Peter* (Moody, 2004), 177.

10 Dennis and Barbara Rainey, *Staying Close* (Word, 1989), 158.

11 Ibid.

12 William Barclay, *The Letters of James and Peter* (Westminster, 1976), 219.

13 David Boehi, Brent Nelson, Jeff Schulte, and Lloyd Shadrach, *Preparing for Marriage* (Bethany House, 2010), 172.

14 Barclay, 219.

15 Tripp, 47.

16 Ibid., 51.

17 Doriani, 120.

18 Tripp, 52.

Chapter 2

1 David Boehi, Brent Nelson, Jeff Schulte, and Lloyd Shadrach, *Preparing for Marriage* (Bethany House, 2010), 103.

2 Ibid., 102.

3 Ibid., 103.

4 Ibid., 38, citing H. Norman Wright.

5 D. Edmond Hiebert, *1 Peter* (BMH, 1984), 196.

6 Ibid.

7 John MacArthur, *1 Peter* (Moody, 2004), 177.

8 Daniel M. Doriani, *1 Peter* (P&R, 2014), 112.

9 Michael Bentley, *1 & 2 Peter: Living for Christ in a Pagan World* (Evangelical Press, 1990), 10.

10 Quoted by Doriani, 113.

11 Hiebert, 197.

[12] "Husband Discovers How His Wife Handled Their Conflicts," *Preaching Today,* Sermon Illustrations. http://www.preachingtoday.com/illustrations/2012/February/7020612.html

[13] Charles R. Swindoll, *Insights on James and 1 & 2 Peter* (Zondervan, 2010), 187.

[14] Doriani, 113.

[15] Hiebert, 197.

[16] J. Allen Blair, *1 Peter: Living Peacefully* (Kregel, 1959), 143.

[17] Swindoll, 187.

[18] John Ortberg, *God Is Closer Than You Think* (Zondervan, 2005), 16.

[19] Warren W. Wiersbe, *Be Hopeful: 1 Peter* (David C. Cook, 1982), 82.

Chapter 3

[1] William Barclay, *The Letters of James and Peter* (Westminster, 1976), 221.

[2] David R. Helm, *1-2 Peter and Jude* (Crossway, 2008), 103.

[3] Juan Sanchez, *1 Peter and You* (Good Book Company, 2016), 115.

[4] Quoted in Sanchez, 115.

[5] D. Edmond Hiebert, *1 Peter* (BMH, 1984), 200.

[6] Helm, 104.

[7] R. C. Sproul, *1-2 Peter* (Crossway, 2011), 95.

[8] Hiebert, 201.

[9] Sanchez, 119.

[10] Daniel Powers, *1 & 2 Peter/Jude* (Beacon Hill, 2010), 108.

[11] Charles R. Swindoll, *Insights on James and 1 & 2 Peter* (Zondervan, 2006), 188.

[12] J. Daryl Charles, "1 Peter" in *The Expositor's Bible Commentary,* Revised edition, vol. 13, edited by Tremper Longman III and David E. Garland (Zondervan, 2006), 328.

Chapter 4

[1] Oliver's Travels, "Guarantee Perfect Wedding Day Weather with Oliver's Travels!" January 23, 2015 www.oliverstravels.com/ (accessed October 11, 2017).

[2] David R. Helm, *1-2 Peter and Jude* (Crossway, 2008), 105.

[3] John MacArthur, *1 Peter* (Moody, 2004), 177.

[4] Dennis and Barbara Rainey, *Staying Close* (Word, 1989), 158.

[5] Ibid.

[6] Charles R. Swindoll, *Insights on James and 1 & 2 Peter* (Zondervan, 2010), 188.

[7] Helm, 105.

[8] MacArthur, 180.

[9] D. Edmond Hiebert, *1 Peter* (BMH, 1984), 204.

[10] Adapted from Rainey, 165.

Chapter 5

[1] Stuart Scott, *The Exemplary Husband* (Focus Publishing, 2002), 59.

[2] R. C. H. Lenski, *The Interpretation of First and Second Corinthians* (Augsburg, 1937), 557.

[3] Daniel M. Doriani, *1 Peter* (P&R, 2014), 119.

[4] Warren W. Wiersbe, *Be Hopeful: 1 Peter* (David C. Cook, 1982), 85.

[5] D. Edmond Hiebert, *1 Peter* (BMH, 1984), 205.

[6] Wiersbe, 85

[7] Dennis and Barbara Rainey, *Staying Close* (Word, 1989), 23.

[8] Ibid.

[9] Fritz Rienecker and Cleon Rogers, *Linguistic Key to the Greek New Testament* (Regency, 1976), 757.

[10] J. Allen Blair, *Living Peacefully: 1 Peter* (Kregel, 1959), 153.

[11] Charles R. Swindoll, *Insights on James and 1 & 2 Peter* (Zondervan, 2010), 190.

[12] See R. C. Sproul, *1 Peter* (Crossway, 2011), 95.

[13] Scott, 201.

[14] Ibid.

[15] Alexander Strauch, *Leading with Love* (Lewis & Roth, 2006), 61.

[16] See Scot McKnight, *The NIV Application Commentary: 1 Peter* (Zondervan, 1996), 193.

[17] Owen Strachan and Gavin Peacock, *The Grand Design* (Christian Focus, 2016), 98.

[18] Wiersbe, 86.

[19] Billy Sunday, as quoted at Preaching Today, www.preachingtoday.com/illustrations/1998/august/5310.html.

[20] Rainey, 203.

[21] Steven Curtis Chapman, "I Will Be Here." Used by permission.

Chapter 6

[1] John Piper, *What's the Difference?* (Crossway, 1990), 11.

[2] Owen Strachan and Gavin Peacock, *The Grand Design* (Christian Focus, 2016), 14.

[3] Ibid., 13.

[4] Piper, 17.

[5] Bonnie Pritchett, "Anti-bullying Bait and Switch," *World Magazine*, September 2, 2017. world.wng.org/2017/08/anti_bullying_bait_and_switch.

[6] Ibid.

[7] Ibid.

[8] Fritz Rienecker and Cleon Rogers, *Linguistic Key to the Greek New Testament* (Regency, 1976), 757.

[9] A. T. Robertson, *Word Pictures in the New Testament*, vol. VI (Baker, 1933), 110.

[10] J. Daryl Charles, "1 Peter" in *The Expositor's Bible Commentary*, Revised edition, vol. 13, edited by Tremper Longman III and David E. Garland (Zondervan, 2006), 328.

[11] Strachan and Peacock, 58.

[12] See Stuart Scott, *The Exemplary Husband* (Focus Publishing, 2002), 263.

[13] D. Edmond Hiebert, *1 Peter* (BMH, 1984), 206.

[14] Adapted from Dennis and Barbara Rainey, *Staying Close* (Word, 1989), 181.

[15] Charles R. Swindoll, *Insights on James and 1 & 2 Peter* (Zondervan, 2010), 190.

[16] See Strachan and Peacock, 59.

[17] Robert Morgan, *Nelson's Complete Book of Illustrations* (Thomas Nelson, 2000), 357.

Chapter 7

[1] Patrick Jackson, "Where There's a Will There's a Whim," BBC News, January 17, 2007. News.bbc.co.uk/2/hi/europe6268015stm.

[2] A. T. Robertson, *Word Pictures in the New Testament*, volume VI (Baker, 1933), 110.

[3] D. Edmond Hiebert, *1 Peter* (BMH, 1984), 207.

[4] Stuart Scott, *The Exemplary Husband* (Focus Publishing, 2002), 170.

[5] Paige Patterson, *A Pilgrim Priesthood* (Thomas Nelson, 1982), 112.

[6] Hiebert, 207.

[7] Wayne Grudem, *1 Peter* (IVP Academic, 1988), 153.

[8] Scott, 196.

[9] L. F. Cervantes, "Woman," *New Catholic Encyclopedia* (McGraw-Hill, 1967), 14:99.

[10] Nick Georgandis, "Man Learns Old Blanket on the Back of His Chair Is a Highly Valuable Antique," diyeverywhere.com/2016/01/24/man-learns-old-blanket-is-worth-nearly-half-a-million-dollars/

[11] Hiebert, 208.

[12] Derek Cleave, *1 Peter* (Christian Focus, 1999), 92.

[13] Robertson, 111.

[14] John MacArthur, *1 Peter* (Moody, 2004), 183.

[15] See John Phillips, *Exploring the Epistles of Peter* (Kregel, 2005), 143.

[16] J. Allen Blair, *1 Peter: Living Peacefully* (Kregel, 1959), 155.

[17] See Charles R. Swindoll, *Insights on James and 1 & 2 Peter* (Zondervan, 2010), 193.

[18] Ibid.